# FOREVER YOUNG

## WWII

### December 7, 1941–August 15, 1945

AN ORAL HISTORY
OF AMERICA'S BRAVE
YOUNG SOLDIERS

# VICTOR L. ROBILIO, JR.

Published by Victor L. Robilio, Jr.

Copyright © 2012 Victor L. Robilio, Jr.

For additional copies, contact the publisher at
P.O. Box 18329, Memphis, TN 38118.

ISBN 978-0615-663562

First Edition July 2012

*The oral history stories in this book were dictated from the Veterans. We do not attempt to correct the context, events, or grammar.*

# TABLE OF CONTENTS:

# PREAMBLE

War is the most abominable thing that nations can do to one another. World War II was a necessary evil to destroy the diabolical and sadistic empires of Japan ("sun flag") and Germany ("Nazi Swastika"). The fact that Hitler's brain was syphilis infected is no excuse. His empire was made up of German New Age vandals.

The Allies did not start winning World War II until the Battle of Midway in June of 1942. Four Japanese air-craft carriers were sunk by U.S. Navy and Marine Corp air power. The same Japanese aircraft carriers that attacked Pearl Harbor on December 7, 1941 were sunk at Midway. Japan never recovered nor smiled again after the Battle of Midway.

The Japanese code of Bushido (honor above life) cost them dearly. Their suicide rule, "Never Surrender" was not of any particular use in modern warfare. It reminds one of the present day terrorist tactics against innocent civilians (vest bombs, truck bombs, etc...). May God save the civilized world from any future tyrants, terrorists, or fascist.

"Real men do shed tears", Winston Churchill openly cried on September 7, 1940 while viewing London's Eastside homes destroyed by 367 German bombers (escorted by 600 fighters). Debauched German Luftwaffe Commander, Herman Goering, drank champagne and picnicked at Normandy, France on that fateful day. This picnic occurred while he viewed his planes leaving for London. Goering was pleased with his "blitz" (fire storm) September 7, 1940. He made two terrible mistakes: He underestimated the British Civilians courage and tenacity. His next mistake was that he switched his "Blitz" from factories and military targets to civilian areas (innocent men, women, and children).

7

Because of the switch, the RAF had time to rebuild and repair its bases. The British factories were spared bombing and thus also increased their production of the Spitfires.

**America's Greatest Generation in 1930.**
*(Courtesy of Vic Robilio)*

**Cecilia Robilio**
*(Courtesy of Victor L. Robilio Jr.)*

# MINORITIES AND IMMIGRATION

May God save us from ever repeating the way that we treated the Japanese American citizens during World War II. Their sons made up the fiercest and one of the best regular fighting army units we had in France. After Pearl Harbor, fear caused our government to lock up tens of thousands of Japanese American citizens in California interment camps. Their eighteen- year old sons were allowed to form the 442 Regimental combat team. They were well disciplined, tough, and very brave. The Germans feared them.

An all black combat unit, the 370 Regiment, 92 Infantry Division, was operating in Italy. They fought against Germany's best troops. A black lieutenant, Vernon Baker, received the Medal of Honor for knocking out German machine gun units near Castle Aghinolfi. He also successfully led the battalion assault on Castle Aghinolfi.

The Italian and Jewish Americans also made up a sizable part of every American combat unit. As I read World War II journals, the Italian and Jewish names "pop up." Regarding the Italians, it is easy to spot them in the text: Gatti, Chiozza, Lucchesi, and Garibaldi. Regarding the Jewish American soldiers (in the journals) it is just as easy to recognize them: Lutz, Silberberg, Magdovitz, and Weinberg.

Now, let's talk about a Latino unit called the "Snake Killers." First and foremost they were usually dropped behind Japanese lines. They were told to "wreck havoc" on the Japanese. Our Latino soldiers were also very useful during the liberation of the Philippines.

The American Indians were ferocious combat troops. They were used for both the European and the Pacific Campaigns. A Creek Indian, Ernest Childers, received the "Medal of Honor" while fighting in Italy.

Today our President and Congress should help the Latinos living in the U.S.A. (10,000,000 plus). They should bring them into our mainstream way of life and out of the darkness. A way to obtain citizenship must be created. They must pay taxes and become skilled workers. This needs to be created by our President and Congress immediately!

Bill Richardson, Hillary Clinton, and Barack Obama all understand our problem. They all three have a heart and soul. The people that hate Latinos are void of God's love. They are using the Latinos as their hate vehicle. They blame them for their own "self-created" personal problems. Let all of us pull together now and get something accomplished quickly for the Latinos.

# LITTLE BOY MEMORIES OF WORLD WAR II

## Journal by *Victor L. Robilio Jr.*

1.) A Navy pilot and his wife stayed at our home in 1942. They needed help. This was when the United States Government was building Millington Naval Air Station, near Memphis, TN. Mom and Dad were very patriotic Americans.

2.) In 1944, a Memphis Ferry Command B24 Airplane ran into trouble over North Parkway and Evergreen Street in Memphis, TN. My parents and I viewed the Army Air Corp. Airmen standing in the plane's doors on North Parkway. They were looking for a "flat emergency piece of land" to set the big plane down on. The plane eventually crashes into some homes on Garland Street near my Grandmother Robilio's home. She and I were standing in the street when it crashed and a huge noise came by us. We became scared and both of us started to cry. The B24 killed two people in the houses it hit, three people in the plane, and demolished three houses on Garland Street.

3.) During the war, my mother said that two Japanese minisubs were captured in St.Louis after passing up the Mississippi River via of New Orleans, Natchez, and Memphis. They were originally dropped off in the Gulf of Mexico by a Japanese submarine, to gather information.

4.) One Sunday, during 1944, I watched captured German P.O.W.'s near Highland Street and Southern Avenue in Memphis, TN. They were in the "L&N Rail yard" riding a train's open box car. They had long German overcoats on and they waved at me. Mom became very angry at me for waving back at them. She told my dad and I, "Those bastards are killing our boys and do not be friendly to them by waving." I later found out that many German and Italian P.O.W's were boarded and fed at Como, MS near Memphis during the war.

5.) The Air Raid Warden, for our area, fussed at my family for leaving a light on during a practice "blackout". This was occasionally done in Memphis. Mom, Dad, and I were all at the Rosemary Theatre watching a movie.

6.) On VJ Day, August 15, 1945, I beat on my bicycle with a large metal spoon to make noise. Two older "bachelors", driving a convertible car on my street, which was Dickinson, told me to shut up my noise making. They hurt my feelings. I am sure that they were unhappy that the "handsome soldiers" were returning to their girlfriends very soon.

7.) Bubble gum was not available during World War II. My dad gave me a box of Super Bubble Gum in October of 1945. I "pigged out" and chewed all 100 pieces by myself. This was to the utter detriment of my teeth!

# Synopsis of the Beginning of World War II

## By *John Robilio* and *Victor Robilio Jr.*

1. 09/01/39—Invasion of Poland by Germany then Russia invaded Poland 17 days later.
2. 09/03/39—England and France declare war on Germany
3. 09/27/39—Surrender of Poland to Germany, Russia occupies Eastern part.
4. 09/27/39-04/09/40—Germany, England and France—Phoney War (Sitzkrieg)
5. 11/30/39-03/10/40—Russian/Finnish War; Russia wins at great cost.
6. April of 1940—Russians execute 20,000 Polish officers in Katyn Forest, they blame the German Army. Stalin gladly approved this order of extermination. He wanted to kill Poland's leaders.
7. 04/09/40—German invasion of Denmark and Norway, Danish resistance lasts only a few days; Norwegians will fight until the end of June but they will surrender.
8. 05/10/40—German invasion of Holland, Belgium, Luxembourg, and France; Holland, Belgium, and Luxembourg will oppose the Germans less than a month.
9. 06/14/40—Paris Taken
10. French will sign an armistice at the end of June. Germans demand large payments from the defeated French but allow the establishment of an independent government at Vichy. Germans occupy sixty percent of France.
11. August 1940—German indiscriminate bombing of RAF Air Fields and shipping lanes in the English channel—convoys, military ships, and harbors of England.

12. 09/07/40—German bombing of London, 348 bombers +617 fighter escorts. The "Blitz" on civilians began late that afternoon.

13. 09/15/40—The RAF wins Battle of Britain preventing Nazi invasion of England. German code name was "sea lion" for the invasion. Performance of the RAF is spectacular- sometimes shooting down German planes at a ratio of 3 to 1. The invasion of England is cancelled. Indefinitely. Frustration relative to England causes Hitler to covet the vastness of the Soviet Union.

14. 10/1/40—Because he cannot invade England, due to the superiority of the RAF, Hitler turns his aggression ideas to the East, dedicating himself to the smashing of the Soviet Union and the destruction of the Stalinist Regime.

15. 06/22/41—German attack upon USSR, the German forces will score staggering successes until 12/05/1941 when the massive Red Army counterattacks near Moscow, Germany is then hammered by Russia's many armies.

16. 7th of December, 1941—Japanese attack U.S. at Pearl Harbor.

17. 01/25/1942—Thailand declares war on the U.S. and Great Britain. Thai military join Japan in an attack on Burma.

18. 04/29/42—Burma taken by the Japanese Army.

19. Germans scorn the neutrality of Brazil and sink Brazilian ships. Anger of Brazilian government reaches a climax in August of 1942. After denouncing the sinking of seven Brazilian ships in August, Brazil declares war upon Germany on August 22nd, 1942. She will send troops to Italy and will aid in the defense of the mid-Atlantic and the South Atlantic. She will play an important role in guarding allies shipments from the Brazilian coast to West Africa. Brazil will represent a vital link in the Takoradi air rout. This route moved supplies from Florida to West Africa and the Middle East via Brazil. Mexico declared war on Germany in May of 1942 due to the loss of her tankers and freighters. She will send food and raw materials to the USA. 14,000 Americans of Mexican origin will see combat

and will play important roles in the Philippines and Formosa theatres of war. A Mexican air squadron will be formed to aid the allies.

20. Chile also declared war on Germany for the very same reasons as Brazil and Mexico and joined the allies.

These are my three reasons for writing this book:
1. Recognize the Vets
2. Inform school children of WWII History
3. Immigration Reform

# Chapter I

# The Story of Staff Sergeant Lester Lowell Braddy: At Bataan and as a Prisoner of War

## Journal by *Sondra B. Davis*

### *The Lost Years*

I am the daughter of a veteran of World War II and I would like to share some of the personal experiences my family endured because of the war. Some of the events of this story were told to me by my mother, Erma Thornton Braddy. She is 91 years old and resides in a local nursing home.

My dad, Staff Sergeant Lester Lowell Braddy, was from Byron, Illinois, and enlisted in the Army Air Force on October 5, 1938, at Rantoul, Illinois. He studied airplane mechanics and instrument work and completed an advance course at Sperry Aeronautics School in Brooklyn, New York. When he met my mother he was stationed at Hunter Field in Savannah, Georgia, with the 48th Materiel Squadron, Air Force Combat Command. The approximate time of the beginning of this story was December, 1940. He was 22 years old and my mother was 27 years old. Mother was divorced with a three-year old son and my dad had never been married.

Mother met my dad when he visited her hometown, Morton, Mississippi, in December, 1940, with a friend from Morton who was also stationed in Savannah. Mother said it was "love at first sight" and on their second date, May 1, 1941, they were married. They returned to Savannah uncertain of what their future together would hold.

In a letter to his parents postmarked October 21, 1941, my dad wrote:

*I was figuring on coming North this Fall to see my beloved folks. But Uncle Sam threw a monkey wrench into the machinery and I won't be able to make it. We have received orders to depart from Savannah the 16ᵗʰ of Oct. for some tropical island and I am just plain heartsick but can't do anything about it…*

*We are leaving this evening at 6:05 by troop train for San Francisco, Calif. and from there we go by boat to the Philippine Islands, as far as I can find out. I have been dreading to write you all as I just hated to think that I was going and tried every way possible to get out of it but just "no soap".*

This was the beginning of a period of life that only those left behind could imagine and never truly know the full extent of the perils and unbelievable hardships these young, inexperienced members of our military forces must have endured.

**Staff Sergeant Lester Lowell Braddy**
*(Courtesy of Sondra Davis)*

My mother and brother moved back to Morton to live with my maternal grandparents, not certain what the future held for them at this point. I was born April 7, 1942, and my dad's death certificate is dated August 1, 1942. He never knew of my birth; all of her telegrams and letters were returned because of the fall of Bataan on April 9, 1942. When my mother met my grandparents in Byron, Illinois for the first time, they also met me. After their marriage they never had the opportunity to travel to Illinois before he left for the war.

My paternal grandparents and mother were informed by telegram dated December 29, 1942, that my dad was listed as a prisoner of war. Then almost a year later the dreaded telegram dated September 12, 1943 arrived from the Adjutant General's office in Washington DC, that my dad had died on September 7, 1943. This information was obtained from the Japanese Government through the American Red Cross. However, this date was later changed by the Department of the Army to August 1, 1942. You will note that for approximately a year they did not know he had died. According to this report, he died of malaria. The letter concluded: "may the thought that he gave his life heroically in the service of his country be of sustaining comfort to you."

Over the years of my childhood I have vivid memories of riding the train from Jackson, Mississippi, to Chicago, Illinois, every summer to visit my grandparents, aunts, uncles and cousins. My dad had three brothers and five sisters so our summers were filled with wonderful memories of our visits.

During the next ten years, I remember very few instances of anyone talking about the war or my dad. Occasionally mother would talk about how much she missed him but never anything about the war and how he died. We continued to live with my grandparents in Morton and mother worked at a café, a "dime store," and later at the local bank. Mother never remarried.

On January 9, 1952, after ten years of persistent communications with the United States Government and the Department of the Army, my mother and grandparents were informed that my dad's body would be transported to Morton for an official military burial service.

I can remember so vividly the service at a small cemetery in Morton of a soldier playing taps, the military gun salute, and the presentation to my mother and me of the American flag that draped the casket. I will always treasure this memory and the honoring of my dad is such a patriotic manner will continue to make me proud to be his daughter.

In January, 2000, I was in California with my husband who was attending a professional meeting when at dinner one night a friend asked if we had read any of Tom Brokaw's books on The Greatest Generation. He had just read The Greatest Generation Speaks: Letters and Reflections. By now he had heard my story about my dad and because I was very emotional and frustrated over my feelings about the war and his death, he offered to send me a copy to read.

At this time, I think I was already beginning to want to know more about World War II and my dad's experiences after viewing the movie "Saving Private Ryan." I cried throughout the movie but for the first time was able to sit through a war movie and understand the horrible reality of the war and possibly why my mom and grandparents never shared their feelings with me. I never watched war movies so this also was a new experience.

In October, 2000, the librarian at the public library in Morton called me. She said that several months before, Mr. Abie Abraham from Renfrew, Pennsylvania donated a book he had written, Oh God, Where are You?, to the Morton Library in memory of my dad. He was on Bataan when my dad was there, experienced the Death March with him, and was with him when he died. The book is an autobiography of his experiences during the war and includes the fall of Bataan on April 9, 1942, his time as a prisoner of war, and his ultimate rescue in 1945. Mr. Abraham wrote:

*I pray this story will in some measure serve as a tribute to those who have died, and to those living who have bore so much.*

*This story wasn't written to bring back sad memories, but as a reminder to the younger generation that freedom wasn't bought easily, but with guts, sweat, blood, and death. Perhaps this story will be a reminder to some of our youth that they will understand a little of what went on.*

One of the most important revelations of Mr. Abraham's book is the fact that he was able to keep such precise and accurate records of people's names, their unit and rank, where they were from, family names, and in so many cases, the exact date, time and place they died.

The book relates to many graphic and painful memories of the Death March and his experiences in the prison camps. It was very difficult to read; however, late one night I read on page 98 the following:

*Lester Braddy was the lookout man. As Father Talbot was praying, Lester would glance at the holy man for a few seconds, then he would gaze out the window. It's a wonder that he didn't get a stiff neck.*

And another meaningful quote:

*Lester Braddy, who was sitting with us, said, "I sure miss my beloved Erma, and can't wait to get back to her and the rest of the family."*

Between the tears of excitement and joy, I now knew someone who was with my dad who experienced the same loneliness, despair, and unbelievable hopelessness my dad must have felt. Mr. Abraham wrote his book because people wanted to know his story and wanted him to share his feelings and experiences through the eyes of the many who never came home to their families and friends. In 1977, this book was published. How very special Abie Abraham is to me. I just wish I had known him 50 years ago. How different my life could have been.

I now have been able to read the complete file my grandmother shared with me shortly before her death in 1972. When my grandmother first gave me these papers it was so traumatic and emotional for me to read that I just filed them away without ever reading the complete file. However, in these documents was a letter that was from T-Sgt. F. D. Lane, dated April 10, 1949, Las Vegas Air Force Base, who was in prison with my dad. The following is a reprint of the letter:

*Your son and I were in the same organization from October 1940 until the fall of Bataan April 9, 1942.*

*He was thought lots of, as he was a good worker and could always be depended on. We were in the same platoon during the months we fought as infantry in the Philippine Islands.*

*After the fall of Bataan I did not see him again until after we had survived the death march to Camp O'Donnell. Therefore we were weakened and starving at the time of surrender; so the death march was just about the finish for all who were on it.*

*The Japs moved us to Cabanatuan in June, 1942. The death rate was terrible so Lester was taken sick about July 4, 1942 and died July 10. I talked with him the day before he passed away, he had no fear of death, but of course he hated to leave his wife and parents.*

*He was buried at Cabanatuan Cemetery in a group, the graves had markers last time I saw them July 4, 1944.*

*Remember that God took him out of his suffering, and those of us who survived are affected in more than one way. Sincerely yours, Duwitt*

His letter gave me some crucial names of the prison camps my dad was in and the exact date of his death. However, this date is not the same date that Mr. Abraham and the United States Government provided us. This is also another instance that I could not understand why my grandparents never shared this letter with me earlier. I wondered, did they ever contact Mr. Lane and if so, did they know first-hand just how much my dad had suffered?

I cannot imagine the many months my mother and grandparents went to sleep worrying about whether my dad was hungry, if he was sick or if he was alive. I thank God everyday for helping me to release the emotions that I had buried for 50-plus years of my life. I am excited about reading books now and talking to veterans and former POW's. It has finally allowed me to have closure to the events leading up to the death of my dad. I only wish this had happened many years ago so I could have asked my mother and grandparents to share their feelings about those years. However, the devastating disease of dementia has robbed my mom of this opportunity.

One of the most significant possessions I have that express the love my dad had for me was shown through the eyes and heart of my mother. She shared the letters where he talked about the baby she was carrying and the love he had for my mother and me. Mother just never shared this with me until after I married, and then it took me years to be able to finish reading them.

Also, he told my mother before he was deployed that if he did not make it back for her to buy me a piano on my sixth birthday and give me lessons. He came from a family who played many different musical instruments and loved to sing and play together every opportunity they had; another wonderful memory of my visits to my grandparents in Illinois each summer. Mother fulfilled this request in the summer of 1948 when she purchased my piano. I took lessons until I graduated from high school in 1960.

As I have expressed previously my life definitely was changing and I knew I wanted to know more about my dad and the war. I knew Mr. Loy Brown, a member of my church, had been a POW in the Philippines and in Japan but until now, he was just a very nice and sweet man I knew and respected. I remember asking him one day if I could come and visit with him about his war experiences. He graciously allowed me to ask some questions and because of his willingness to share some very painful memories, I finally knew face-to-face someone who had been in the war.

Since he also served in the Pacific Theater and he specifically spent some time on the Philippine Islands, he knew about Camp O'Donnell and he was actually a prisoner during some of the time my dad was at Cabanatuan prison camp. Through his eyes I was also able to experience what my dad endured. He did not know my dad personally but the stories he told me of his experiences, I knew my dad just might have walked by him sometime or they might have been in a room together. Mr. Brown was transferred to a prison camp in Japan. How very special and what a caring friend he is to the many people who love and respect him for the sacrifices he made for America's freedom.

In the fall of 2001, I was contacted about another war orphan living in Tupelo, Mississippi, Adrian Caldwell. She invited several other sons and daughters of veterans who served in WWII to her home for a visit. I attended this meeting and for the first time in my life (at age 59), I met other people who has lost their dads to the horrors of the war, and I could finally relate to their pain and sadness. I began to heal my emotions as I shared for the first time the story of my father and the love I had for him. It was an experience

**Staff Sergeant Lester Lowell Braddy (left)**
**and Erma Thornton Braddy**
*(Courtesy of Sondra Davis)*

that I will always treasure and I look forward to meeting other "orphans" and sharing our stories. She told me about the internet access for the American War Orphans Network (AWON) and I have joined this wonderful organization.

I did not write this story for sympathy. I wrote it for my mother and the memory of my dad and the many families who were affected in such a manner that it took someone like Tom Brokaw to finally "unlock" the floodgates of grief and frustration, and to help people understand how proud America is for the young men and women who gave their lives so we could have the freedoms that I hope we do not take for granted.

I am a charter member of the National World War II Memorial that was completed in 2004 in Washington, D.C. honoring these brave heroic men and women. How very proud it made me feel when I toured this beautiful memorial and I was able to read my dad's name in the Registry and witness the awesomeness of the meaning of its creation. I can finally say thank you dad for your tremendous sacrifice and for the memories, however sad and painful they are. I now know just how much I miss him and how I would have loved being his daughter and experiencing his arms holding me and loving me, but I know my Heaven awaits me someday where we will all be together forever.

Sondra Braddy Davis
Daughter of Staff Sgt. Lester Lowell Braddy
48th Materiel Squadron, Air Force Combat Command

# To the Veterans of World War Two

They leave us daily now
These brave old men of World War Two
Whose sacrifices humble us
With both grief and gratitude

Grief for their lost youth
For their unsought journey into hell
For their friends and comrades
Whose rest is final

Gratitude for their selflessness
For their pride of country
For their pressing on in battle
In spite of fear

And when we think of them
As we often should
We shall remember
And say a prayer, and weep


*by Anne M. Robilio*
**9/26/98**

# CHAPTER II

# THE CAPTURE OF ROME

## Story of *Abraham "Doc" Pepper*

It all started at Monte Casino. The 88th Infantry Division (the Blue Devil) took a lot of shrapnel from the Allied bombs that were dropped. The Allies were trying to dislodge the Germans on top of Monte Casino. The Allies finally took Monte Casino. On the attack line, the French Moroccans were on the right side; on the left side was the 92nd Division (a black division); and "Doc" Pepper was with the 88th

**"Doc" Pepper (far left) Italy, 1944**
*(Courtesy of "Doc" Pepper)*

Division (the Blue Devil) which was right in the middle. Doc said that the black soldiers from the 92nd Division saved his life more than once. The worst battle was held near Monte Casino at Santa Maria where 1,500 pieces of field artillery were fired at the Germans. "Doc" told me that this was the worst battle he was in, during his entire career. Abraham "Doc" Pepper was with the 105 field artillery unit.

The allies finally decided to send French Moroccan troops to "mop up" Monte Casino at 2:00 a.m. in the morning. The Moroccans used flame throwers and their bolo knives to enter the ruins of the monastery and get the Germans out of there and eliminate them.

Italian partisans with mules moved "Doc's" unit over the mountains, upon reaching the valleys the Germans were then shelled heavily by "Doc's" 105 Howitzers.

The 88th Division moved down Highway 6 to capture Rome. The Luftwaffe hit his column and he had to jump into a ditch. Five men of his unit jumped on top of him and two were already underneath him. Two German tanks came out to meet them and the 88th Division immediately blew them up. The date was June 6, 1944.

"Doc" Pepper was searching a vacant building in Rome when four civilian dressed Gestapo agents attacked him. They knocked his steel helmet off and hit him in the head with a sledgehammer handle. A 88th Division comrade soon found him bleeding badly on the floor. He was rushed to the Rome hospital and stitched up.

The 88th Infantry Division got two to three days of leave in Rome and they got cleaned up, drank plenty of wine, and finally had good food. "Doc's" unit was chosen to represent the American Army to meet with Pope Pius XII at a private audience. He blessed "Doc" which helped him in future combat battles. "Doc" Pepper also met with a Jewish Rabbi, and also many other Jews, and Allied flyers that the Pope had hidden in the Vatican from the Germans. The recent Anti-Catholic lies that have been told about Pope Pius XII are false. According to Abraham "Doc" Pepper, an eye witness, the Pope did shelter Allied flyers, Jews, and Rabbis'.

Abraham "Doc" Pepper was 87 years old as of April 23, 2008. He passed away on July 19, 2008. He will always be remembered!

# Chapter III

# De La Salle College, Manila February 12, 1945, 2:00 pm

## Story of *Bestial Japanese Marines*

January 9, 1945 was the "beginning" of the end for the Japanese occupation of Manila. The 6th Division, 37th Division, 40th Division, and 43rd Division of the United States Sixth Army landed at Lingayen Gulf. By February 3, American Army troops reached the northern suburbs of Manila.

The American troops who captured the Christian Brothers, De La Salle College, in Manila stood shocked. The time was 4:30 pm, February 15, 1945. What they saw turned their stomachs upside down. "Korean born" Japanese soldiers and Japanese Marines had bayonet to death sixteen Christian Brothers and twenty-five civilians (women, men, and children). They left them there to bleed to death and die with no help for over three days.

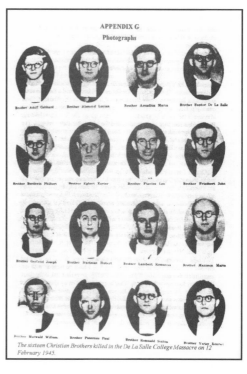

APPENDIX G
Photographs

Brother Adolf Gebhard  Brother Alemund Lucian  Brother Arcadius Maria  Brother Baptist De La Salle

Brother Berthwin Philbert  Brother Egbert Xavier  Brother Flavius Leo  Brother Friedbert John

Brother Gerfried Joseph  Brother Hartman Hubert  Brother Lambert Romanus  Brother Maximin Maria

Brother Mutwald Willam  Brother Paternus Paul  Brother Romuald Statius  Brother Victor Xaver

*The sixteen Christian Brothers killed in the De La Salle College Massacre on 12 February 1945.*

three days. The Americans took pictures of these war crimes. The

Survivors said that the Japanese had attempted to violate the women as they bled to death. Brother Baptist De La Salle saved the life of a little boy, Jose Carlos Jr. He placed the child under a mattress until the Japanese left. Then, the child found safety in a dark cellar where the Japanese could not see him in the dark. Among the hand full of survivors, Father Cosgrave later stated that it all started after lunch on Monday, February 12, 1945.

Nine days before this sad event two motorized units of American tanks and trucks moved through North Manila carrying troops. The Americans liberated five hundred captured Allied Civilians at Santo Thomas University, this was on February 3, 1945. Japanese guards on the University campus (a Japanese prison for American and Allied civilians in North Manila) were astonished when five American tanks broke through the gate.

*Photo taken by the Americans as they entered the college on Friday, 15 February 1945, in the afternoon. The door to the wine cellar (above) was open. Several bodies lay one on top of the other. The body on the left (foreground) was bloated.*

**De La Salle Feb. 15, 1945**

*(Courtesy of These Hallowed Halls)*

## DE LA SALLE COLLEGE, MANILA
## FEBRUARY 12, 1945, 2:00 P.M.

31

The city was totally surrounded and other American troops were moving up from the South. They encountered very stiff resistance in South Manila. The Japanese Marines panicked and were filled with anxiety and fear. Since 1942 they had treated the citizens of Manila harshly and bestially. Fearing a full scale uprising and unable to fight both the Manila citizens and Americans at the same time, they went crazy. Japanese General, Tomoyuki Yamashita, did not try to control his officers and/or troops. So, Manila was treated bestially with wholesale destruction, rape, murder, and pillage. Over 90,000 Filipino Citizens died because of inhumane treatment during this time and the years of Japanese wartime occupation. Some of the Japanese officers were executed for war crimes by the Americans after the war.

*(Courtesy of Earl Harrell)*

# Chapter IV

# The B17 "Screwball" Express

## Story of *Sam N. Reaves, Jr.*

Sam Reaves grew up in North Memphis on Breedlove Street. He moved to Whitehaven, which is a part of Southwest Memphis. He attended Whitehaven High School. Sam joined the Army Air Corp. in 1944 and did his basic training at Keesler Field located near Biloxi, MS.

**Sam Reaves**
*(Courtesy of Sam Reaves)*

After becoming an Air Corp. Sergeant he was assigned to a B17 as a "ball turret gunner." His crew picked up a new B17 at Savannah, Georgia. They headed for England by way of Fort Dix, New Jersey; Banger, Maine; Goose Bay, Labrador; Reykjavik, Iceland; and Wales, England. He said that they developed engine and brake problems after leaving Labrador. Sam said that they needed repairs which delayed their trip for an additional thirty days. Their final destination was an airfield forty miles north of London, near Kimbolton Castle.

Upon arrival Sam's squadron was told they had to give a maximum effort. They would have three days of combat flying and then have three days off for rest and relaxation (R&R).

Thirteen planes made up a squadron, three squadrons made up a maximum effort group. Sam would fly between 10,000 and 30,000 feet. Outside temperatures would reach between -35 degrees and

-40 degrees: He was required to wear a electrically heated flight suit, gloves, and a warm hat.

His very first target was Hamburg, Germany. His 379th Bomb Group, 527th Squadron of the 8th Air Force was targeting key industrial cities for carpet bombing. GI's on the ground, fighting in Germany, could see their contrail or vapor trails- condensation behind their B17's four engines. Seeing this gave them hope that the end of Hitler's folly was near.

Sam's last flight was aboard the Screwball Express. It was a borrowed B17 from another bomb group. The date was April 15, 1945. His original plane had engine starting problems. His crew was late in taking off and missed the group's rendezvous site near Paris, France. By flying alone and with no P51 escort, the Screwball Express was in harms way. Ingolstadt, Germany was the group's target.

Sam's plane was shot down near the French Army's battle line inside Germany. He bailed out and was shot at in the air by friendly fire from our French Allies. They were Moroccan troops. The co-pilot, Martin "Killer" Kane, was killed because his parachute never opened. He was from Chicago. The pilot, Joe Hurtal, hit a tree because his parachute did not fully open. He was from New Jersey. He lost the use of his feet permanently.

The only pleasant thing about landing, Sam remarked was "The Moroccans ran off some pitchfork carrying German peasants who would kill him." They also gave him a bottle of cognac and regretted shooting at him. Also, he found an American Burial unit nearby that was from the 142 Infantry, 36th Division, U.S., 7th Army. They fed Sam and his fellow crew members, and gave them shelter.

Some survivors were: Donald S. Miller, the tail gunner from Vancouver, Washington; John D. Roberts, the radio operator; Carlos A. Whitehead, the nose gunner (Togglier); and Richard Rowan.

# Chapter V

# The Surrender of Chichi Jima

## Story of *Warren Jordan*

Warren Jordan was a seaman, 1st class, in the U.S. Navy during World War II. He was aboard the Destroyer, the John Tripp, for two years. He boarded the ship at New York harbor.

The John Tripp operated out of Saipan and Guam (in the Marianas group of islands). It had a crew of 326. Its biggest weather challenge was the typhoon that hit the American and Japanese fleets during August of 1945. The captain had to keep the ship pointed towards the winds and the huge waves of the typhoon. The John Tripp looked like a submarine as she was pounded by the huge waves. Warren said, "she was as much under the waves as she was above them." Our U.S. B24 bases on Okinawa and our B29 bases on Saipan were all devastated. Smaller war ships were popped into two sections. Planes were turned upside down. The typhoon scattered both the American and Japanese fleets and sunk some warships.

The John Tripp had no chaplain aboard. Warren Jordan was asked by the captain to be the chaplain. He agreed to this and did a great job for Catholics, Jews, and Protestants. There were no atheists in combat during World War II, they all converted and believed in God soon after combat started.

In August of 1945 the John Tripp received a message to go from Guam to the island of Chichi Jima and ask the 40,000 Japanese there to surrender. Chichi Jima is the largest of the three islands in the chain, called the Bonin Islands. They are found north east of Iwo Jima. When Japan surrendered in August of 1945 the empire was so large it took weeks to get to all of the Japanese held territory. The island of Chichi Jima was bypassed for two years by General McArthur, in his island hopping campaign. With 40,000 troops and many deadly 15 inch shore guns Chichi Jima would be very inhospitable to any invaders.

The John Tripp entered the pristine harbor and dropped its anchor. The Japanese commander was stubborn and would not believe that the empire of Japan had surrendered. He was a friend of the Emperor's first cousin.

The U.S. captain met with the Japanese commander on the John Tripp three times over a period of three weeks. The Navy would not go ashore for fear of being held hostage. A Japanese garbage scow was sent into the pristine harbor to pick up the John Tripp's garbage. Warren said that a Japanese spy, who attended UCLA, was aboard the scow. He listened to the crews talk and gossip. Warren was trying to swap him cigarettes for his very nicely carved decorative Japanese waist knife. Warren thought that the spy did not understand English and said to him, "I would be shooting you if it wasn't for the surrender in Tokyo Bay." That's when he told Warren about attending UCLA.

A complete B26 was lying on the beach shot down. The Japanese said all died in the crash except for one, and he died a few days later. Some of the crew felt the Japanese, who were starving, may have cannibalized them.

Sam Cox, an American Army Guerilla, told me that he had found starving Japanese in New Guinea and killed them. He said that they were eating an Australian soldier in the jungles of New Guinea.

Every time the John Tripp moved in the harbor, the 15 inch shore guns followed her. Finally, after the radio aboard the ship communicated with someone who he trusted, the Japanese commander surrendered. The crew of the John Tripp finally went ashore to collect souvenirs. Each crew member received one Japanese Marine Rifle as a souvenir, there were 326 crewmen.

Warren Jordan was discharged at San Diego on his ship's return to the United States. Later on, the old destroyer, the John Tripp, was used to test the atomic bomb in the Pacific at an island test site called Bikini Islands.

## The Banana Tree

The Destroyer Tripp was anchored off of the coast of Saipan in a harbor near a white sand beach with bananas trees on it. Warren Jordan told the executive officer that he could see some bananas, through his field glasses, growing upside down. The field officer sent Warren, one Navy rifleman, and the chef of the ship (with a machete) onto the beach in a small wooden whaler's boat.

The chef got on top of the tree and started to cut down the bananas. Warren was collecting the bananas and the Navy man was guarding the situation. The Navy rifleman, who was trigger happy, started shooting at the tall grass along the beach which the wind blew in. The chef thought the Japanese were attacking. This scared the chef and he accidentally cut his arm open from top to bottom with the machete. Warren quickly wrapped a tunic around the chef's arm to stop the bleeding.

The three men finally made it back to the boat. They took the chef to a Navy hospital ship that was luckily nearby. The result of all of this concludes Warren Jordan's life lesson- Never take a trigger happy person with you on an excursion. The ship almost lost it's chef!

## Spring of 1945- Near Okinawa

Warren Jordan was on "spotter duty." The John Tripp and two other U.S. destroyers were guarding the large U.S. Air Craft Carrier George Washington. The Washington was just a sitting duck that was lying in the water.

Warren spotted three circling Japanese Betty Bombers with his long range Navy glasses, they were eight miles away. Two of the three immediately dived at the U.S. Carrier, George Washington. The John Tripp notified the captain of the Washington what was coming straight at him. He opened up with his five inch cannons. Warren watched the two Betty Bombers (kamikazes) being hit. They were vaporized by the Washington's 5 mm cannons.

The third Japanese Betty Bomber changed his mind and headed straight for the John Tripp. It looked like a canoe compared to the George Washington. The Japanese pilot made a valiant run. Warren could "see death" coming straight at the John Tripp. At the last thirty seconds, before collision, two five mm cannon shells exploded under the Betty Bomber and shrapnel killed the Japanese pilot. Warren watched "death" barely miss the flag mast of the John Tripp and crash about 100 yards in front of the ship.

## *Biography, Written by: Warren Jordan*

Warren Jordan has called Memphis home for almost 90 years. Originally born in Pennsylvania, he and his family moved to

**(L to R): Ed Myrick, Warren Jordan, Victor Robilio Jr.**
*(Courtesy of Victor Robilio Jr.)*

Memphis, TN when he was just two years old, growing up as a dedicated southerner.

Warren graduated from Tech High School, obtained an LLB Degree from Memphis University of Law School in 1940, received his License to Practice Law in 1947 and received a JD Degree from the University of Memphis in 1963.

In 1940 the E.I. Dupont Co. contracted with the government to build a munitions plant north of Memphis called the Chickasaw Ordnance Works. Warren was among the first men employed on this project serving as Personnel Director. After a short time, Dupont transferred Warren to Illinois to work as the Personnel Director with the Kankakee Ordnance Works, which was an enormous plant manufacturing T.N.T. and other military explosives.

Warren joined the U.S. Navy in 1944 and served aboard a destroyer in the Pacific. Our country was at war and in those years most men preferred the battlefield to home front duty.

Returning home safely, Warren found the business world more appealing than practicing law. With so many men and women returning to the work force, Warren organized several personnel employment agencies. Deciding to branch out and start his own business venture he created International Chemical Corporation, an automotive aftermarket supplier and product manufacturer. One of Warren's favorite interests has been the Memphis Union Mission where he served on the Board of Directors for 18 years. He is also an active participating member of First Baptist Church located at Poplar and Parkway.

He retired as Board Chairman of International Chemical Corporation at the age of 85. Warren recently passed and will always be remembered for his bravery. Warren once told me that we will never experience a vast military world war again: "Vic, it will be a war against civilians. May we avoid it, please!"

*(Courtesy of Warren Jordan)*

# CHAPTER VI

# THE REPLACEMENTS

## Story of *Ed Myrick*

At the beginning of World War II the drafting, the training, and the deploying of American Naval, Marine, Army, and Army Air Corp. personnel was a problem. Production of planes, tanks, ships, supply trucks, and other war supplies and materials was solved by our enormous "free enterprise" manufacturing ability. Ford, General Motors, and Chrysler made no civilian cars during the war. Their production was converted to Army and Marine tanks, trucks, armored personnel carriers, jeeps, etc...

Replacements of old destroyed equipment; the improved fire-power of new tanks, new planes, and artillery gave us the edge over the enemy in fixed battles. Improved ship sonar and radar and better communication systems all helped us defeat the Germans and Japanese.

Last, but not least, were our human replacements. They won the war. We had huge casualties in 1944 and 1945. This was both in the air and on the ground: killed, wounded, sick (frost bite and jungle rot), and missing in action (M.I.A.).

My friend, Ed Myrick, entered the Army Air Corp. in March of 1945. He received his basic training at Wichita Falls, Texas. Ed was trained to be a remote control turret mechanic for the B29 Bomber. He was trained for electrical work. Ed was a replacement for a B29 ground crewman who could be a casualty during the Fall of 1945 invasion of Japan.

The last five months of the war in Europe was a replacement nightmare. Many American battle units were made up of fifty percent new replacements. This was the situation by May of 1945. In the Pacific Theatre the battles of Iwo Jima, Okinawa, the Philippines, and New Guinea were also replacement nightmares.

Ed Myrick and hundreds of thousands of other replacements were ready to step into the shoes of fallen comrades. Thank God for Harry Truman and the Atomic Bomb that stopped the Japanese War of aggression against the Allies.

Ed finished his course training the first of November 1945. Thanks to all the replacements like Ed, who were ready should we have needed them.

# Chapter VII

# The USS Arkansas and the USS Idaho Battleships

## Story of *Tom Miller*

**Tom Miller**
*(Courtesy of Tom Miller)*

Tom Miller went to Memphis Technical High School from 1936-1939. He volunteered after graduation for the Navy in July of 1942. Tom was trained at Norfolk, Virginia Naval "boot camp."

In September of 1942, Tom was sent to the new Millington Naval Air Station located near Memphis, TN. This was Tom's first assignment.

Tom was then sent to the Brooklyn Naval Yard, in 1943, to join a bunch of "Yankee sailors" aboard the USS Arkansas. He was one of a few Southerners aboard. The others aboard the ship thought that Tom was stupid because he talked slow. Tom "played possum" with them and cleaned most of them out in card and poker games. The "Yankees" had no money left for shore leave.

The "old" Arkansas had a teak wood deck. She had been built in 1905. The Arkansas was the guideship for many Allied Convoys to England. She was slow but formidable looking with her twelve inch guns.

Tom was aboard the Arkansas June 6, 1944 as the Arkansas shelled the German held coastal defenses at Normandy. He watched the slaughter on Omaha Beach. The Arkansas received gunfire from German coastal guns at Omaha Beach. A brave U.S. destroyer captain came in dangerously close to the shoreline and took out the German coastal guns. The Arkansas "burned up" its twelve inch guns firing on the German positions. It had to return to Boston, Massachusetts to be refitted with new twelve inch guns.

In late 1944 Tom went through the Panama Canal on the Arkansas. He was part of an anti-aircraft element soon to join the battleship Idaho. Tom was transferred to the Idaho, which was newer, faster, and bigger than the Arkansas. We gave the old Arkansas to our ally, Russia.

Aboard the Idaho, Tom viewed the raising of the American flag on Iwo Jima in April of 1945. He witnessed the brave Marines battling from his position on the deck of the Idaho.

In August of 1945, the Idaho was sent to Tokyo Bay to be next to the Missouri for the Japanese surrender. Tom said, "The Japanese came aboard the Missouri wearing stove pipe hats." He witnessed the surrender. McArthur was very brief and the Japanese dignitaries signed their papers quickly.

Tom said, "Tokyo Bay and its surroundings were extremely quiet." The Japanese were very, very quiet in ending this horrible and unconscionable war that they themselves had started! One could not even hear a dog bark in Tokyo.

**Betty and Tom Miller**
*(Courtesy of Tom Miller)*

# CHAPTER VIII

# THE PHILIPPINES, LEYTE

## Story of *Earl Harrell*

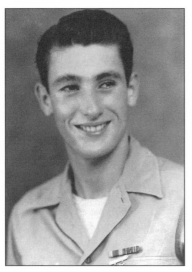

**Earl Harrell**
*(Courtesy of Earl Harrell)*

Earl was transported to Leyte in the Philippines by the Army in 1945. He was sent as a replacement.

Earl's 200 man combat unit was a heavy weapons company. He specialized in the machine gun and mortar. Earl was a member of the 24th Infantry Division, of the U.S. 6th Army. Earl said that every fourth rifle company was a heavy weapons company.

Leyte Island was invaded by the U.S.A. on October 22, 1944. This is where Earl's 24th Division fought valiantly. They campaigned against the Japanese 35th Army. The city of Tacloban was located on the big island of Leyte. Tacloban was the capital of Leyte.

Earl said that the 24th Division had 3,500 killed during the first six weeks of fighting. He recalled they had around 12,000 wounded or missing. The Japanese losses were a staggering 70,000 casualties (killed, wounded, or missing). The carnage on both sides was absolutely horrible. The Army's 24th Division was called the "Victory Division."

Earl found a Japanese helmet in the mud near a machine gun pill box. He also found remnants of a shot down American airplane nearby. Earl told me, "I found the rubber heel of an American Airmen's shoe near the downed plane."

Earl became sick with Malaria and Jungle Rot in early August of 1945. He was sent to a "Mash" hospital on the outskirts of the city of Tacloban on the island of Leyte.

Earl said that his ration was thirty bottles of beer a month. Refrigeration was scarce so he let the Air Corp. chill it on their high altitude patrols.

The Japanese were still fighting in the Leyte Mountains three weeks after their August 15, 1945 surrender. We were still dropping pamphlets on the small islands to get the holdouts to surrender.

Earl was transferred to a Signal Corp. unit for the last three months of his stay in the Philippines. He helped guard a lot of Japanese prisoners from the bypassed islands that finally surrendered. We had to carry them back to Japan on our ships.

A terrible typhoon hit Leyte and dropped six inches of rain in November of 1945. Earl's duty with the Signal Corp. before it hit was to get the Japanese prisoners to cut down all the coconuts on nearby trees. They could become "cannonballs" during a high wind typhoon (200m.p.h.).

Earl was finally shipped back on the U.S.S. Saugus, a L.S.D.-4. There were still Japanese mines in the waters near the Philippines. Earl remembers the mines being exploded by a U.S. naval gun from the Saugus.

There were fifty pregnant American nurses and Red Cross workers on the top deck of the U.S.S. Saugus. The ship's sailors told Earl that they were too friendly with the Army officers and were being shipped home. They also said some nurses were being dishonorably discharged.

The U.S.S. Saugus arrived in Oregon in December of 1945, a full five months after the Japanese surrendered. Earl got ten days leave and returned to his hometown to visit his family.

Earl was then sent to Kennedy Hospital in Memphis, TN for further medical treatment. He also went to another hospital in Florida for medical help.

Earl Harrell's service records were accidentally burned up in a St.Louis warehouse in 1946. Today, Earl and his wife reside in Olive Branch, MS.

**Earl Harrell**
*(Courtesy of Earl Harrell)*

UNITED STATES OF AMERICA
OFFICE OF PRICE ADMINISTRATION

№ 817650-FB

O.P.A.
VALID
U.S.A.

## WAR RATION BOOK No. 3

Void if address and Sign altered

NOT VALID WITHOUT STAMP

Identification of person to whom issued: PRINT IN FULL

Harry          E          MARIANI
(First name)      (Middle name)      (Last name)

Street number or rural route 250 Stewart Ave

City or post office Garden City  State L.I. N.Y.

| AGE | SEX | WEIGHT | HEIGHT | OCCUPATION |
|-----|-----|--------|--------|------------|
| 6 | Male | 79 Lbs. | 4 Ft. 8 In. | Student |

SIGNATURE  Mrs. E. Mariani

(Person to whom book is issued. If such person is unable to sign because of age or incapacity, another may sign in his behalf.)

### WARNING

This book is the property of the United States Government. It is unlawful to sell it to any other person, or to use it or permit anyone else to use it, except to obtain rationed goods in accordance with regulations of the Office of Price Administration. Any person who finds a lost War Ration Book must return it to the War Price and Rationing Board which issued it. Persons who violate rationing regulations are subject to $10,000 fine or imprisonment, or both.

OPA Form No. R-130

### LOCAL BOARD ACTION

Issued by _____
(Local board number)          (Date)

Street address _____

City _____  State _____

_____
(Signature of issuing officer)  Bnh Y

---

**4**

206 245 CV

UNITED STATES OF AMERICA
OFFICE OF PRICE ADMINISTRATION

# WAR RATION BOOK FOUR

OFFICE OF PRICE ADMINISTRATION
OPA

Issued to  HARRY F. MARIANI
(Print first, middle, and last names)

Complete address  250 STEWART AVE

GARDEN CITY  NY

### READ BEFORE SIGNING

In accepting this book, I recognize that it remains the property of the United States Government. I will use it only in the manner and for the purposes authorized by the Office of Price Administration.

*Void if Altered*  _____
(Signature)

*It is a criminal offense to violate rationing regulations.*

OPA Form R-145                    16—35570-1

## War Ration Book
*(Courtesy of Harry Mariani)*

# CHAPTER IX

# 706TH ORDINANCE, L.M. COMPANY, 6TH INFANTRY DIVISION

## Journal by *Stan Caummisar*

**Military Record of Earl Stanley Caummisar, Sr.**

**Army Serial Number 35487835**

**First Combat**—Maffin Bay, Papua, New Guinea, June 1944-August 1944. The Sixth Infatnry Division made an amphibious assault against moderate Japanese resistance. The mission was to eliminate enemy opposition and secure an area of approximately 200 square miles on which to build new airstrips. Aircraft from the new fields could bomb and strafe Japanese shipping and strongholds and provide air cover for future amphibious assaults.

**Stan Caummisar – New Guinnea 1944**
*(Courtesy of Stan Caummisar)*

**Second Combat**—Sansapor, Dutch New Guinea, August 1944-January 1945. An amphibious landing was made against strong opposition. Our mission was to secure a large beachhead, then advance northwestward toward strong Japanese fortifications (for two years the Japanese had dug tunnels into the highest hills, some 175-200 feet high, dismantled artillery pieces, re-assembled them on rails inside the tunnels). Heavy fighting occurred for approximately six weeks when the Sixth finally took the hills. The few remaining Japanese filed along the coast toward Sorong, and some fled to the mountains where they lived with the aborigines.

**Final Combat**—Participated in an amphibious landing at Lingayen Gulf, Luzon, Philippine Islands, on January 9, 1945. Our company landed at H+10 minutes, in the second wave. Fortunately, opposition was extremely light, since the Japanese left only a rear-guard to harass the American forces.

After 219 consecutive days of combat (without relief), fighting through cane fields, around airfields and reservoirs, and over mountains, the Sixth Infantry Division concluded its combat on August 15, 1945, with the surrender of the Japanese. When the cease-fire order was issued, the Sixth Infantry Division was the most heavily engaged Division in the U.S. Army, facing the last large groups of organized enemy in the Pacific War.

## *New Guinea- Earl Stanley Caummisar*

Here, really is where my story begins. As a member of the Combat Ordinance Team, I was called upon to help retrieve the disabled tank and, if possible, return it to the Ordinance Shop for repairs. So, our Team mounted a huge tank retriever and lumbered slowly along the path blown in the rain forest by leading tanks.

We reached the disabled tank without incident, but it was necessary to turn the huge tank retriever around before latching on to the tank. If you can picture that monstrous piece of equipment almost surrounded by trees and undergrowth you can imagine the difficult task facing us. We would cut some small trees and vines, the driver would drive forward a few feet, cut the wheels and pull forward again. After fifteen or twenty minutes the driver had maneuvered the retriever to a point where he was perpendicular to the path.

At that point all hell broke loose! The Japanese had zeroed in on the disabled tank before we arrived. They waited until the retriever was in a position where it could not be driven away quickly, then, began dropping artillery shells on our position. We scattered like chickens, running in every direction. Running as fast as we could through the undergrowth. I was a few steps behind a big farm boy from Iowa as we broke out of the brush into a clearing. Our momentum carried us for perhaps thirty yards before we realized the clearing was an airstrip, and we were completely exposed.

We didn't have much time to correct our mistake because the Japanese on the farside of the airstrip immediately cut loose with machine guns. That big old farm boy from Iowa used his head that day- and, in doing so, probably saved my life. He threw up his hands and fell forward as though he was hit. Seeing him, I, too pretended to be hit and fell forward. Then the firing ceased. We laid there for what seemed like eternity- but it couldn't have been more than five or ten minutes. An infantry platoon moving along the path, cleared by the tanks, had heard the machine guns moved cautiously to the edge of the airstrip.

Seeing our predicament, and after a few whispered words of instruction, the entire platoon began firing across the airstrip to keep the Japanese pinned down while my friend and I inched ourselves backward on our stomachs to the safety of the trees. The tank and the tank retriever had both received direct hits, so we were forced to walk back to our bivouac empty handed.

Another story of New Guinea. I was on an ammunition detail on the beach. There was a long coconut jetty or pier jutting out onto the bay. As we watched a PT boat pulled up to the far end of the pier.

A lone Naval Officer emerged and started walking toward us. As he neared us his face seemed familiar and finally it dawned on me. Here was Bernie Crimmins, a schoolmate at St. Xavier High School in Louisville- 2000 miles from home and we meet on a pier. I guess Bernie was as amazed as I that we met so far from home. He said that he was running low on fuel and hoped to find some at Maffin Bay. We drove him to the Fuel Depot.

One rather amusing thing happened on Luzon in the Philippines. Delbert Sparks and I were "buddies" and never more than ten yards from each other. One night a fire-fight broke out on the perimeter of our bivouac. We both grabbed our carbines and hurried toward the gunshots. When we neared the fight we both dropped to the ground behind trees until we determined where we could be most helpful. It was not until then that either of us realized Sparkie was completely nude. No clothing, no shoes or socks. No Nothing!

Today, Stan is alive and well in Memphis, TN.

**Stan Caummisar and Family**
*(Courtesy of Stan Caummisar)*

# CHAPTER X

# WASP (WOMEN AIR FORCE SERVICE PILOT)

## Story of *Frankie Yearwood*

Frankie was the "last lady pilot" in the last graduating class of the WASP. She graduated from Sweetwater, TX flying school. Frankie flew the PT-17 Stearman, a double wing plane; the AT6, the Texas Trainer; and the BT13. General Hap Arnold gave the flying wings to her.

She was stationed in Sweetwater, TX. The AT6 was a "work horse plane." It was used all across the country. Frankie towed air targets for pilots in need of practice. They would shoot at them using electrical circuits. No bullets were used at all.

Frankie was enlisted from March of 1944 until the end of the year. She was asked to fly people on short trips. This system helped to keep our men pilots in combat.

Frankie was discharged in late 1944 and tried to get a ride by air to Memphis where she lived. Cargo planes carrying supplies to the Memphis Army Depot were grounded because of bad weather. Frankie finally got a ride on a very slow train from the Texas coast to Memphis. It stopped at all the tiny towns that it passed through. She finally caught a ride by car at midnight with some newly discharged black servicemen. They were kind to motor her by car to Memphis. This good deed saved her from the slow train from South Arkansas to Memphis.

Currently today there is a WASP museum located in Sweetwater, TX. Frankie is no longer with us and she is greatly missed.

**Uncle Silvio Robilio (center)**
*(Courtesy of Danny Walker and the Warren Walker Family)*

# Chapter XI

# A Living National Treasure

## Journal of *Jim McCauley*

Most people go through life and never discover a Treasure. I am proud to say that I have discovered a National Treasure on a small island in central Florida. I am not the first, nor will I be the last, to discover this wonderful treasure. Hidden away on the small island of Siesta Key, just south of Sarasota, Florida is a fairly unknown National Treasure that my wife and I have discovered. This hidden Treasure is Captain Ralph Emerson Styles, United States Navy (Retired).

Captain Ralph lives alone in a one story gray clapboard house with bright yellow awnings at #99 Beach Road. The house was probably built in the fifties or sixties, but Captain Ralph is a little older than his house. He lives in Florida during the winter months and moves to his permanent house in Maggie Valley, North Carolina during the summer months.

Captain Ralph was born February 27, 1910 at home in Asheville, North Carolina. That means in about three years, Ralph will hit the 100 mark. Ralph's father was a descendant of John Stiles who was awarded a homestead in Western North Carolina near Cherokee after the Revolutionary War. Captain Ralph graduated from Asheville High School in 1927 and attended Weaver College and the University of Tennessee before entering the U.S. Naval Academy in 1929, graduating in 1933. He was assigned to the command carrier, The USS Lexington and in 1937 attended Submarine School. On December 7, 1941 he was assigned to the USS Narwhal and was in Pearl Harbor serving as engineer officer. Captain Ralph survived because he was in his apartment having breakfast when the Japanese surprise attack was launched. After Pearl Harbor he was in two war patrols and the Battle of Midway. In 1943 he was ordered to command the USS Sea Devil, a submarine which was completed and commissioned in 1944. After three war patrols in the Pacific he received two Navy Crosses, Legion of Merit and Navy Unit Citations.

There is much more to his war history and his long time service to his country, but the real story is Captain Ralph today. He has not been commissioned or ordered to perform his current self-appointed duties. But, he performs his patriotic duties today, and every day. He performs these duties out of pure love of his country and his deep appreciation for all who served their country in military service.

In January my wife and I were honored to meet and assist Captain Ralph in his daily duties, at his home on Siesta Key.

It was around 6:30 PM. My wife and I were sitting on our beach patio when other renters at our condo complex approached us and introduced themselves. They were five couples from the Missouri boot hills. One asked: "Did you attend the flag ceremony tonight?" Our answer was "no" and what flag ceremony were you talking about? "Oh the one down the street, the one that people attend at sunset everyday." To tell the truth it sounded a little "touristy" to us. When the neighbor from Missouri continued to explain, I could hear the emotion in his voice and just how serious he was. "You will never experience an event that will impact your soul as much as this one will", he said. Obviously we became more curious and the next evening at 5:15 PM we strolled down the beach, camera in hand, to witness the event. People were gathering on the corner, across the side street from Captain Ralph's home. The public beach was directly across the street from his home. You can tell Captain Ralph because he was surrounded by fifteen or twenty people who were listening to his greetings and he was wearing a baseball hat that said "USS North Carolina" and a white satin bomber's jacket with his name on the upper left side. The back of his jacket showed several "Rising Sun and National" Japanese flags. Later we found out that these were the Japanese ships he sunk as Captain of the USS Sea Devil.

As I approached the group people started introducing themselves to me, as if I just stumbled into a family reunion. They were from New York, Wisconsin, Michigan, Pennsylvania, Ohio, and other northern states where the weather was much colder. I was the only one from Mississippi. I then turned to Captain Ralph Emerson Styles, he smiled, took my hand and said: "Were you in the service?" "Yes sir", I answered, "the United States Air Force." The next words out of his mouth will stay with me the rest of my life. "Thank you so much for the service that you gave to your country, it's people like you that make the difference." I'm not sure if I answered him or not, I was mesmerized by this man, this National Treasure.

As more people gathered, a man came down the sidewalk with a drum hanging from his neck. A woman appeared with a bugle and Captain Ralph said loundly: "It's time. Fall in by two's!" There was a man standing next to me from Ohio, he looked at me and said: Well, I guess we "fall in." "I guess so", I answered. There we were, ten rows of two, waiting for our commands. The beat of the drum started and Captain Ralph stood at attention in front of his new command and shouted: "Attention!" It was a natural reflex when the entire group of vacationers snapped to! "Forward March!" was the Captain's command, with the voice of authority. Our vacationing "band of brothers" marched in cadence across the street to Ralph's corner. When we reached his sidewalk he shouted "column right!" And every person knew exactly what to do. We felt like we were marching in the Macy's Thanksgiving Parade. It is amazing how your natural instincts take over, it took me back forty five years. After we took a "column right!" we marched about ten feet and the captain commanded: "column halt!" Then, "column Left!" We were now facing the flagpole. "Flag attendants to the Flag!" he commanded. Two women stepped up to the flag pole and started lowering the American Flag. At the same time, the woman with the bugle marched to the middle of the front lawn and played the most touching rendition of Taps you have ever heard. I don't know how many dry eyes there were in the column, but mind wasn't one of them. I had a hard time even breathing. I kept telling myself, pull yourself together, you can't break down and cry in front of all of these people. The flag was lowered, folded in military style, and the triangle folded flag was presented to Captain Ralph. He then turned to the column and shouted "column right!" Then, "forward march!"

We marched to his front porch. "Column halt!" Captain Ralph marched alone to his front door and laid the flag just inside. Standing on his front porch he commanded: "Parade rest!" The lady with the bugle marched to his side. He then announced: "For all those who lost their lives aboard their submarines, play Amazing Grace!" The bugle lady poured Amazing Grace right out of her heart and we all sang, even the people across the street on the beach. "Now, he announced, for all the people who served in the United States Navy. He paused, looked out into the crowd and asked every Navy person to hold up their hands. A few hands went up and he said: "Thank you very much for your service to your country," He turned to the bugle lady and said: "Now play Anchors Away for the people who served in the Navy." We all sang "Anchors Away." He went through the entire branches of the service. Next was the Army, he asked for hands and a few went up, he thanked them and we sang "As the Caissons go Marching Along." Next was the Air Force, I held up my hand, I was the only one in the crowd. He looked right at me and in a most sincere voice said: "Thank you for your service to your country." I almost lost it, I had to swallow several times to hold it in. "For the Air Force, play, Off We go into the Wild Blue Yonder." The group sang. I couldn't open my mouth, my eyes were so filled up

I couldn't even see Captain Ralph. Then on to the Marines where he thanked them and we sang "To the Halls of Montezuma."

Captain Ralph marched off the front porch, assumed his position in front of the column and ordered: "About face!" We turned like professionals, like we did many years ago. "Forward march!" We marched. "Column left!" we turned left and marched back across the street. "Column halt!" With the look of a commanding officer he said: "Thank you again for your service and the sacrifice you made for the country, column, dismissed!" It was his final order. We all stood frozen as if we weren't really dismissed and we didn't want to make any mistakes.

The flag ceremony of Captain Ralph Emerson Styles was over, but no one really wanted it to be over. We all stood around like school children waiting for there parents to pick them up after school. I have never felt so proud of my country or proud that I served in the United States Air Force. In fact, I haven't thought about serving in the Air Force for many years. Captain Ralph changed all that and I'm sure he has changed many lives with his nightly ceremony. For all of you who served, you should know that every night, in Captain Ralph's front yard, across from the beach in Siesta Key, there is a National Treasure who is thanking you for your service to your country. Thank You, Captain Ralph Emerson Styles. U.S. Navy, retired. Well, not really retired.

Sadly, Captain Ralph Emerson Styles passed away on October 7, 2008.

..........................................

Jim McCauley lives in Oxford, MS. Born and raised in Southern Indiana and a product of Indiana University. His professional career includes the US Air Force (Texas, New Mexico and Spain), the United States Jaycees Executive Officer, and retired after 27 years as a Corporate Executive with the International Holiday Inn Corporation. His lifetime involvement with community involvement included founding membership of committees for "Special Olympics" and "Give Kids the World" (a partner for Make a Wish) headquarters in Florida. In retirement he is an author and playwright. His first novel, "Pinpoint Inc." was published in November of 2006.

Email: Jimcc@mindspring.com

**Captain Emerson Styles and Jim McCauley (right)**
*(Courtesy of Jim McCauley)*

# Chapter XII

# The Liberators Brought Back History

## Journal by *Lester Gingold*

Ken Burns asked WWII veterans to stand for recognition at the recent preview at the Germantown Performing Arts Center of his PBS special that begins airing in late September. In a packed theatre less than two dozen joined me in rising to the occasion. Ken reminded the audience that WWII veterans were dying at the rate of 1,000 a day, and how important it was to record our histories and memories for future generations.

**Lester Gingold**
*(Courtesy of Lester Gingold)*

"My dear liberators" begins a letter I received from Carla Gast Kemper, a Dutch girl of 19 who had been imprisoned by the Nazis as a penalty for helping American pilots escape from Holland. In a prison camp in Germany when we liberated her, the first request I was able to provide was a toothbrush and a green leather jacket I had taken from a German home. She had been unable to brush her teeth for six months and was extremely cold. We corresponded for years after the war. Carla later married and raised a large family and travels extensively in Europe.

This is one of my favorite war stories. After landing in LeHarve to await transportation to the front lines, I shook hands with Gen. Dwight Eisenhower, who was visiting the troops. I leaned down from a truck and he smilingly shook my hand.

Later we boarded freight cars (the old 40-and-8s) for our trip across France. In WWI, the box cars were 40 men or eight horses. Little did I realize a relic idea from 1914 was still effective. There were eight of us in a box car with only straw on the floor. The train would stop in small villages and the French would bring us bread and wine to go with our C-rations. I think of this every time a freight train goes by and I patiently wait for the gates to go up.

Shortly after the close of war in Europe, we were awaiting assignment to Japan or elsewhere, and I was in Mannheim, Germany. A friend rushed in one day to say a general had been in an automobile wreck, some five or six blocks from the hospital where we were billeted. With my trusty small camera, I went to the accident scene just as the ambulance was pulling away with Gen. George Patton, the victim. Within minutes a wrecker was on the scene to haul away Patton's car and the 2 ? ton truck. I had looked in the large car clearly marked with the general's stars on the license. I saw two bottles of whiskey on the floor of the back seat, where Patton had been riding. The car driver was not injured and neither was the truck driver. I took pictures of the Patton car, the truck and the somewhat disheveled corporal who had driven the truck. Prints of these pictures are now in the Patton Museum in Los Angeles.

A few weeks later, I went to Patton's funeral in a small but beautiful church in Heidelberg, sitting on the front row in the balcony. It was only later that I found out my wife Joyce's uncle Col. "Red" Slocum had been Patton's intelligence officer in his African campaign.

While in college at Birmingham-Southern, I volunteered for the Army, and could not pass the eye exam. I was determined, and with a copy of the eye chart at home, memorized all of the letters, and passed with flying colors on a second try. When we were shipping overseas at New York's Port of Embarkation, I was retested, but unfortunately they had a different chart. I convinced the examiner that although my eyes had slipped badly since I joined the army, I wanted desperately to go with my fellow soldiers in the combat engineers to England and the war. They relented, and so my two years in Europe were a reality.

While a senior in college, our nation was involved in the sale of War Bonds. This was a rallying cry to pay for the war and it met with tremendous success. I originated a College War Bond Breakfast and we sold over $15,000 in bonds. That may not sound like much today, but to college students this was a big undertaking. Congratulatory letters poured in from the secretary of the treasury, senators, congressmen and civic leaders. Other colleges picked up the torch, including Princeton and the University of Michigan.

My story will not be on PBS, but I commend the series to our readers. It is an important documentary that will certainly be another award winner for Ken Burns.

**(L to R) Joyce Gingold, Kay Robilio, Lester Gingold**
*(Courtesy of Lester Gingold)*

# Chapter XIII

# The Pineapple Express B26

## Journal by *William S. Norred*

### *Bio*

William S. Norred, native of Pine Apple, Alabama, was born April 6, 1917. He is the youngest of ten children born to Mance and Bernice McKee Norred. He is the last living member of his family today and turned 91 on April 6, 2008.

Mr. Norred graduated from Moore Academy in 1936. He received an athletic scholarship to Troy State Teachers College (now Troy University in Troy, Alabama). Norred won the designation of being the All-

**William Norred**
*(Courtesy of William Norred)*

State Center of the Alabama Intercollegiate Athletic Association for 1939-40. He played on the Troy varsity for three years and was alternate captain of the football team for his senior year. He also played varsity baseball and basketball while a student at Troy. He graduated in 1940 with a Bachelor of Science degree.

Mr Norred began his teaching and coaching career in September of 1940 in Headland, Alabama. In 1941, he accepted a position as Head Coach at Luverne High School in Luverne, AL. By December 7, 1941 (Pearl Harbor), he was ready to prepare to serve his country. (He had previously signed up with the Army Air Corps.).

Coach Bill Norred arrived in California on December 12, 1941, and became Cadet Bill Norred in the United States Army Air Force. He was assigned to Hemet, CA. for primary, then on to Lemoore, CA. for basic training, and finally to Victorville, CA. for his advanced-training. Upon graduation, Norred received his second lieutenant bars and silver wings of a pilot. He then received orders on July 20, 1942, to Barksdale Field in Louisiana.

The 319th Bomb Group was activated on June 26, 1942. It was composed of four squadrons: the 437th, 438th, 439th and 440th. Norred was a member of the 437th Squadron. At Barksdale Field, Lt. Norred began training to fly the twin-engine B-26, Martin Medium Bomber. On August 8, 1942, the 319th Bomb Group was moved to Harding Field, Baton Rouge, LA, and began a 24-hour-a-day ground and air training, in preparation for the real test of combat. By September 6, the Flight Echelon began their movement to Baer Field, Ft. Wayne, Indiana, which was to be their point of debarkation. The 319th Bomb Group was in route overseas.

A total of 57 crews and aircraft were assembled at Baer Field to process for the movement to England via Presque Isle, Maine; Goose Bay, Labrador; Bluie West, Greenland; Reykjavik, Iceland; Prestwick, Scotland and on to London, England.

From England, Norred reported for duty to Telergma Air Base, Algiers, North Africa, in October of 1942. Captain Norred's forty bombing missions were in the Tunisian, Sicilian, and Italian Campaigns, wherein he and his crew won fame in their "Pineapple Express" B-26.

Bizerti, Salerno, and Rome were the scenes of Captain Norred's most hazardous and valuable flights. Captain Norred described the anti-aircraft defense of Bizerti as the fiercest encountered. In his case, however, the toughest assignment was that of giving air support to Lieut. Gen. Mark Clark's Fifth Army at Salerno. "We were in the air three straight days," he said, "Sometimes we flew two missions in a single day." On July 19, 1943, Captain Norred successfully led the first ever raid on Rome. He was Flight Commander for the 108 B-26 bombers, escorted by 100 P-38 fighters. They completely destroyed the Ciampino Airdrome. **

During his African assignment Captain Norred was Flight Commander for 36 of his 40 bombing missions. He had a total of 1300 flying hours, of which 180 were combat hours. He derives considerable satisfaction from the fact he never lost a plane behind him. That means that he led his formations through flak so adroitly that none of the planes was mortally hit. He and members of his crew came through without casualty. Captain Norred received the European-African-Middle Eastern Medal with three Bronze Stars for Air Offensive and the Air Medal with seven Oak Leaf Clusters.

Captain Norred completed his required forty missions in September of 1943. He was returned to the States in October. In December, he arrived in Del Rio, Texas (Laughlin Field) as flight test engineer officer, supervising four officers and 400 enlisted personnel. While stationed there, he met Doris Simmons of San Antonio, Texas. They were married on June 30, 1945.

**Postscripts: I understand the Germans were eating lunch and most of their planes were parked on the runways. This was "payback time" from Allies to the Luftwaffe. – by Victor L. Robilio Jr.

## *Raid on Rome*
## *July 19, 1943*
### By Capt. William S. Norred

The first ever raid on Rome was made by three of the four squadrons of B-26s of the 319th Bomb Group. Since I was assigned Flight Leader of this mission, the following is my first-hand account.

This massive raid of the Ciampino Airdrome, which is a few miles south of Rome, was planned to take out the German facilities and aircrafts based there. Prior to the raid, those aircrafts were strafing and bombing our recently arrived troops in the boot of Italy. They desperately needed our air power to help.

Each of the three squadrons consisted of 36 B-26s, totaling 108 aircraft. We were escorted by 100 P-38 fighters. Because of the importance of this bombing mission, a higher-ranked officer was required on board. Therefore, my co-pilot, Lt. Eugene Early, was replaced by Major Carlisle who explained that he was there only as an observer. The target was three hours flying time from our bases in Algiers. When we arrived over the target and leveled out, my bombardier took over, releasing our bomb load. The other B-26s followed suit. The airfield was full of parked planes and the Germans were in line for their "chow". The sudden appearance of 108 American bombers took the enemy by surprise. The enemy planes, along with all facilities, were completely destroyed. All of the 108 planes made it safely back to our bases.

We American fliers had been warned in advance that Axis propagandists would claim the Americans would attempt to destroy the Holy City's churches. Those claims were false. The raid was considered a huge success. Lt. Roy C. Brown, flying as observer in Capt. Hall Lawson's B26 wrote, "…the coverage by our bombs was terribly accurate." I believe our bombing raid was a "turning-point" in the war because of the major loss of enemy planes.

## *My Biggest Decision on a Raid*
### By Capt. William S. Norred

On December 15, 1942, our target was El Acuina Airdrome at Iugis, Tunisia. This was the eighth mission for the 319th Bomb Group. We had been in active combat since November.

Major Ellis E. Arnold, Jr., was pilot of the lead plane. Major Arnold asked me to fly on his left wing. I was honored to be flying on the wing of a high-ranking officer. At that time, I was a second lieutenant. Before we left the base, Major Arnold asked, "Norred, you gonna stick with me?" And I replied, "Like glue!"

After dropping the bomb loads, our seven B-26s were to loop back over the Mediterranean to return to base. Suddenly, my top turret gunner reported seeing Major Arnold's plane, having been hit by flak, crashed into the Bay of Tunis. I banked my plane to the left and the other five planes followed suit.

We six landed safely back at base, mission completed. The crews all gathered to report for de-briefing by the C. O. who wanted to know how we lost Major Arnold. The only explanation we could come up with was that he apparently made a second run over the target to observe the damage. By then, the sky was full of flak. The C.O. commended us on returning to base, saving our planes and lives.

Postscript: Major Arnold's B-26 Marauder was discovered in November of 2000, during dredging of Tunis Harbor by the Tunisian government. The remains of Major Arnold and his five crew members were positively identified more than two years later. On May 23, 2003 which would have been Major Arnold's 84th birthday, he was buried with full military honors at Hillcrest Cemetery in Goodman, Mississippi.

**Mr. and Mrs. William Norred**
*(Courtesy of William Norred)*

# CHAPTER XIV

# THE BRITISH NAVY PILOT

## Story of *Derek Rooke*

Derek was a teenager when the war started. His family had a second home in Liverpool. One inconspicuous day the Germans hit Liverpool with fourteen air raids in a twenty four hour period. The people of Liverpool had no subways, so they slept outside the town in fields during the "Blitz." Also, food and fuel rationing was another way that the British survived.

Derek was visiting his uncle one week, in Liverpool, when his uncle asked him to deliver some milk early one morning. When on his Uncle's milk route he reached a home on "Queens Drive" (a green parkway) a 12' and 4' German bomb (a river mine) was dangling above the front door (tap, tap, and tap). It was hung up on its own parachute. The bomb was supposed to be a ship mine for the river and port of Liverpool. Derek immediately ran to get a "bomb team" to disarm the bomb. It could have taken out four city blocks had it exploded.

Derek was a pen pal to Miss Louise Pankey of Lagrange, TN., USA. He married her, after a courtship, in 1942. She came over to England by way of a convoy ship and stayed in England during the war. What a courageous lady!

Derek told me that he and Louise walked five miles to a dance one summer in the Lake District of England. The mountain people at Stanford had clogs on and did a lot of swinging when they danced. He also mentioned the Dales people to me who lived nearby.

Derek said he got four times more training than a German pilot. He was General Mont Battan's airplane pilot for his Lockeed Electra Airplane. This plane was used for Mont Battan's trips to India. Derek had met Mont Battan earlier at Inverness, Scotland.

Derek said the British Navy had 2,000 pilots but they were forced to use old American planes. The RAF got all of the new American planes.

Derek served on six British Aircraft Carriers. He was a "top gun" and helped school new British Navy recruits. He said that while in combat "German Bullet Tracers" helped him maneuver our of their tail attacks on his plane. Derek could locate them by tracer direction.

Derek's career took him to the Northwest of Scotland, to the Orkney Islands, and also to Norway. He attacked German shipping, ground troops, and U boats that surfaced. He would first strafe the U Boat and then a slow British bomber would blow it up.

Derek also had joint training exercises with the Russian Air Force. Some storms in the cold North Sea were so severe that his carrier pitched five to seven times before he could land on it. His carrier hook always caught his plane when he landed in the rough weather.

He also viewed a German jet traveling at 500 miles per hour. Derek participated in D Day air attacks. A German Foker-Wulf 190 attached his American made Grumman fighter plane repeatedly, but without any success.

The most humorous story that Derek told me was about golfing at Kirkwall in the Orkney Islands, Scotland. This was the golf course of the "midnight sunsets." He had enjoyed his night 8:00 p.m. T- Time and played nine holes. Upon return to his British Aircraft carrier, the Captain wanted to see him. To his chagrin, Derek had inadvertently borrowed the Captain's golf clubs!

# CHAPTER XV

# ROMANIA'S PLOIESTI OIL FIELDS

## Story of *Brad Bradshaw*

Today, Brad lives in Parkville, Maryland. I have interviewed him twice over the telephone.

Brad did his "Air Crewman" training at Maxwell Field which was located in Alabama. This took approximately two months to complete. Then, he did his "Primary Training" at Arcida, FL. Next, Brad did his "Basic Training" at Gunnerfield, AL. Finally, he did his "Advanced Training" at Columbus, MS.

**Brad Bradshaw**
*(Courtesy of Brad Bradshaw)*

Brad was a co-pilot at first. He picked up his Liberator B24 at Westover Field in Massachusetts in the fall of 1944. His crew flew the new B24 to the Azores, which was located off the coast of Africa. Then, they proceeded on to Marrakesh which is located in North Africa. He reached his Army Air Corp base at Foggia, Italy with "no hitches". Brad joined the 456 Bomb group, 746 Squadron of the "mighty" 15th U.S. Army Air Corp. This was during the fall of 1944.

As I said earlier Brad started as a co-pilot, and then became a 2nd Lieutenant Pilot. Brad's 2nd combat mission was the German's oil refinery at Ploiesti, Romania. His bomb group divided into two parts. Brad was part of the 2nd group. The first group carried 300 pound bombs to start the refinery fires. Brad's 2nd group carried single cluster bombs to produce an oil field inferno.

Brad had been looking for his fighter plane escort. All of a sudden his group was surrounded by P51's with red tails and red propellers. The famous Tuskegee Airmen escorted his group to Ploiesti, Romania.

The B24's attacked at 1,500 feet above the ground. A "V" formation was formed on one level with all of the planes. This type of formation permitted Brad to safely drop his cluster bomb. The single cluster bomb separated about fifty feet, below his plane, into six bombs. His group released all cluster bombs at one command. The ensuing inferno destroyed the Ploiesti Oil Fields. No future raids were needed.

German anti-aircraft 88's hit the gas tanks of some of his B24 group. The B24's that were hit would blow up or implode. Some of Brad's group's planes did not get hit at all. A few were damaged and lost an engine but still made it back to friendly lands. Most of his friends made it back to their base at Foggia, Italy with him.

Brad was in combat from September of 1944 until March of 1945. He completed thirty five combat missions. This is equivalent to fifty regular missions.

**Brad Bradshaw**
*(Courtesy of Brad Bradshaw)*

## *The Story of Bud Dudley*

I interviewed Bud Dudley September 9, 2002. The distinguished founder of the Liberty Bowl passed away on June 17, 2008. The following are my written recollections of that interview.

Bud received the Distinguished Flying Cross, the Air Medal with six clusters, the Campaign Medal, and Battle Stars. He also received the Freedom Foundation Medal. He wrote a book titled, "ETA, used by the Army Air Corp. navigator schools during World War II. "ETA" means estimated time of arrival.

Bud was an excellent B24 liberator navigator. He did some training in Cuba. His crew liked to take R&R at Sloppy Joe's restaurant in Havana, Cuba.

He was eventually assigned to the 15th Air Force. They were stationed at a base near Foggia and Canosa di Puglia. This is an area located in Southern Italy.

Bud completed fifty four missions of ten hours or more. His most difficult mission was the bombing of the Ploiesti Oil Fields in Romania. It was the "most fortified" Allied target in all of the European Theatre during World War II. It bristled with German 88's (Flak guns) anti aircraft guns. German fighter planes (M.E. 109's and Focke-Wulf 190's) were stationed nearby the oil fields.

Hitler's tanks depended on these oil fields for their fuel. The 15th Army Air Corp. was asked to knock them out. Bud's plane was repeatedly hit but they dropped their bomb load. Four of his crewmen were killed and Bud had to bring her back to the base near Foggia, Italy. Bud was truly a "Humble Hero." His sister was the one that told me what actually happened. In my interview Bud only told me that it was a maximum effort by the 15th Air Force to cut off Hitler's fuel supply. I believe this effort helped us win the "Battle of the Bulge." As you and I recall, the German tanks ran out of fuel in Belgium in December 1944.

**Hitler Inspecting His Troops**
*(Courtesy of Carolyn Tipton)*

# Chapter XVI

# The Free French Navy Cruisers: Bertin & Terrible

## Journal of *Charles Jacquard* as told to his son, *Roland Jacquard*

Charles Jacquard was born in 1921. He was living near Lyons in the South part of France. [In 1941 they called that area Vichy France.] That year he decided to join the French Navy at Toulon on the Mediterranean sea.

Later he left the port of Toulon to be assigned as a gunner on the Bertin, a Cruiser of 620 sailors, a ship that was cruising the South Atlantic, on the latitudes of Senegal and Virginia, and eventually stopping in Philadelphia,

**Charles Jacquard**
*(Courtesy of Roland Jacquard)*

Pennsylvania U.S.A. The main role of this ship was to detect German submarines and ships, but also to transport allied troops from Moroccan and Algerian colonies for the coming battle of Monte Cassino in Italy. Eventually moved from the Bertin to a lighter Cruiser, the Terrible (320 sailors ) in July 1944, Charles participated in the Provence recapture that started on

August 15th, 1944. For several days, the Terrible was firing on the German defense along the Coast, while at night they would retract to the Corsican Coast, a safer heaven from the German warplanes.

The next mission of the Terrible was to guide the Richelieu, a much larger ship, from Toulon to Suez in Egypt. On return to Toulon, Charles had his first "vacation" after 3 and half years aboard ships: 10 days to go and see his family. Traveling up north on cargo trains, fueled by wood coal, and trucks it took a long 40 hours to cover the mere 220 miles and reach Lyons.

On Christmas Eve 1944, the crew of the Terrible was partying in Naples bay with some pretty good food and a double allocation of wine.

On Christmas day 1944, everything was normal, with the usual cleaning of guns and the rooms. The Terrible departed for Genoa around 4p.m. About 2 hours later, while having a snack in his enclosed quarter, Charles felt a violent impact on the ship, but had no idea what was going on. He emerged from the quarter (2nd quarter) to find out that a torpedo had hit the nose of the ship, site of his neighboring 1st quarter from which 40 sailors went to their

**Charles Jacquard**
*(Courtesy of*
*Charles Jacquard)*

deaths. There was no time to feel frightened, but the submarine was already long gone. Slowly the Terrible returned to Naples, and eventually, to Tunisia for repairs. Before she was set to sail again, the Germans surrendered August 15, 1945. Years later, and every time that an impact of any sort would happen (such as a hammer hitting the ground), Charles would stress, subconsciously remembering the German torpedo moment that occurred on Christmas day of 1944.

# Chapter XVII

# The Saving of a Little French Jewish Angel

## Story of *Jeannine "Smid" Paul* *(Smeed)*

The time was May of 1940. Jeannine "Smid," her brother Leon, her mother Rachel, and her dad Abraham were living in Paris, France. The German army had just invaded France through Holland, Luxembourg, and Belgium. They punched a hole fifty miles wide in the 9th French Army's defensive lines. Fast-moving German panzer tanks separated the French Army, the Belgium Army, and the large British expeditionary force. To their chagrin, the French

**Jeannine Paul and Ike Smith**
*(Courtesy of Jeannine Paul)*

had not held back any reserves to plug up the fifty mile wide hole. The 9th French Army was mostly made up of colonial troops from French colonies. It was also augmented with draftees from France itself. The German tanks ran about the French land unopposed. French troops and French citizens were frightened by the fierceness of the German attack which was mostly made up of the fast moving German tanks.

The city of Paris was in Grave peril. The Smids fled aboard a train towards the Loire Valley and the safe city of Orleans. The train was shelled and bombed. Jeannine spent her tenth birthday in some woods of a heavy forest near the disabled Loire Valley train.

The evacuation of Paris only complicated the military situation. The "rumor – panic" of German airplanes bombing Paris never materialized. French roads and railroads were clogged by the flee- ing 9th Army French troops or citizen refugees trying to avoid the clash of the two armies.

Ten-year-old Jeannine and her family were caught up in the "death" of this misled French Republic. The death was caused by the "arrogant" Huns and the unprepared French military leaders. The elected French political leaders were also inert.

Jeannine's dad, Abraham Smid, died in the panic driven evacu- ation of Paris. What a horrible thing to happen and be viewed by a ten year old girl. Adolph Hitler and Heinrich Himmler were truly "beasts of death." The sad three member family of Smids returned to Paris after the French surrendered to Germany in June of 1940. Hitler was delighted and surprised at the collapse of the 9th French Army and the lack of sufficient French reserves. Winston Churchill was astonished that the French Army held back no reserves and had to capitulate. Some of the French military and political leaders were incompetent.

In 1942, Heinrich Himmler, a Hitler puppet, (with Hitler's bless- ing) decided to kill, by gas chambers, all the Jews that were left in Europe. He and Hitler were truly "mad men." German Catholic schools were closed the next year in 1943. Many priests and nuns were also arrested in 1943. They were like the Jews, targeted for extermination in death camps.

Jeannine's brother, Leon Smid, was picked up in an I.D. check one morning in 1942. The Gestapo said that he was to be deported. He was finally found in the Paris memorial archives, which has his record of what happened to him. Her brother died at Auschwitz Concentration Camp (the Germans changed his name to Schmidt). This also happened to some American airmen who were shot down over the Channel Islands between France and England. Perhaps someday their mystery will be solved.

The "pick up Jews" raids usually started at 5:00 a.m. They increased "tenfold" in 1942. Always unwanted and uninvited, two Gestapo and two French policemen (or more) would show up. Jeannine said it was very frightening for a twelve year old, hazel eyed, auburn haired Jewish child. One morning at 5:00 a.m., two French policeman and two Gestapo arrived at her door to pick up Jeannine and her mother. One German said, "There is no way we can take such a cute little French girl, let's leave her and take only her mom." The "duped" Frenchmen piped in: "We agree, she is too cute!" Those were the "saving words" for Jeannine Smid.

Jeannine's mother was told to pack her things. Jeannine was only twelve years old and tried to go with her mother to the police station. Her mother told her to go to her friend Rachel's home. In the home there was an eighteen year old Jewish girl and a seventeen year old Jewish boy. Their parents had recently been deported and sent to a concentration camp. The girl was immoral and permissive with German soldiers. Jeannine told a third generation Jewish girl (her friend at school) about the situation. The girl's mother, Mrs. Cohen, took Jeannine in for a while. Eventually, her mother became fearful of the Gestapo and turned Jeannine over to the French Underground. Madame Milhaud (Meo) was their leader and she saved over 500 Jewish children. She worked with Mrs. Charles DeGaulle in this operation. Madame Milhaud was married to a doctor.

Jeannine was taken to Lille, France. She went to a Catholic church. Her papers were falsified in October of 1942. She became a French Catholic teenager, Jeannine Brunet, on paper. A French lady, Tati, helped her with this process. The Gestapo was fooled!

The Nazis continued their "round up" of French Jews. The "round ups" targeted 1st, 2nd, 3rd, and 4th generation Jews. They checked papers on the street and increased the 5:00 A.M. raids.

Jeannine was taken to the Preventorium Trelon School for girls and boys. It was located near Lille, France. She said that about a dozen Jewish teenagers were mixed in with the Catholic teenagers. All the Jewish girls had forged identification papers. The Gestapo never came to the school.

In 1944, Jeannine heard the Allies' artillery pushing the Germans out of France. She watched the long trains and truck convoys of German Soldiers moving in an Easterly direction. The Allies did not even stop to check out her school. However, one morning Jeannine woke up unexpectedly and saw the roof smoldering. A German 88 anti-aircraft shell had gone through the roof of the attic. It was already spent, but its heat could have caused a fire. Jeannine alerted the schools principal and they put water on the smoldering wood. God must have awakened Jeannine that morning because it saved the whole building from burning. By this time, unknowingly to Jeannine, her mom had been killed by poisonous gas at Auschwitz concentration camp.

Jeannine's first cousin, Isaac (Ike) Smith, was stationed in West Germany with the United States Army after Germany surrendered on May 15, 1945. He came to Paris on his leaves to look for Jeannine. He always went to the old neighborhood and asked questions in Yiddish. He could not speak French. A Jewish lady, in the old Paris neighborhood, gave him the name of a lady who knew the location of the boarding school where Jeannine was living. This kind tip led him to the boarding school where he found Jeannine in October of 1945. Jeannine arrived in New York City in 1947 at the age of seventeen. She got a job at a factory while she lived with Ike's family.

Today, Jeannine is living peacefully in Memphis, TN. Jeanine is an artist. She was at first reluctant to speak to me about her "saving." I am delighted that she is speaking out now. This action will help us in America to protect our racial and religious minorities. Religious beliefs should stay out of politics. Our Constitution should be followed to the letter. Thomas Jefferson said, "Freedom of religion; freedom of the press; freedom of person under the protection of the habeas corpus; and trial by juries impartially selected, I deem [among] the essential principles of our government, and consequently [among] those which ought to shape its administration."

Adolph Hitler (1889-1945) destroyed Germany's Judiciary, her freedoms, and her conscious. This happened when Paul Von Hindenburg (1847-1934) made him chancellor in 1933.

**Jeannine Paul**
*(Courtesy of Jeannine Paul)*

**Queen Elizabeth**
*(Courtesy of Dan McCarthy)*

# CHAPTER XVIII

# THE U.S.S. ST. LO (CVE-63)

## Story of *Ed McAteer*

The Battle for Leyte Gulf was also called the "Battle of the Bull's run." Admiral William Halsey Jr. ("Bull" Halsey) made a tactical mistake by following a Japanese decoy fleet. He did not check with his immediate superior Admiral Chester Nimitiz, of NCPAC. Halsey took all of our battleships and heavy cruisers out of the San Bernardino Strait and left it totally unguarded. He went on a "wild goose chase" after the Japanese decoy fleet, on the night of October 24-25, 1944. Taffy 3, the small escort carrier group made up of destroyers and small Casablanca-class escort carriers, were no match for the Japanese cruisers and battleships with 15 inch guns. The Japanese also introduced the Kamikaze death plane during this crucial battle.

Ed was listening to the Grand Ole Opry radio, from Nashville, TN, the morning of October 25, 1944. That morning he had been briefed of the Japanese fleet approaching the unguarded San Bernadino Strait. This was the day that his ship was sunk. He saw the Japanese Kamikaze sweep down and hit the St.Lo's flight deck. Ed was on the deck close enough at impact to see the dead Japanese lieutenant "shoot" out of his cockpit and across the flight deck on impact. He immediately evaporated from the heat of the explosion. The fearless Japanese pilot was reported to be Lieutenant Yukio Seki.

The Kamikaze caught the St.Lo crew refueling and rearming their aircraft. Ed jumped from the flight deck to the focisle deck which was the gun turret deck, to avoid the intense fires. Ed

**85**

severely sprained his ankle from the jolt of the jump. This deck was approximately thirteen feet below the flight deck.

One hundred and forty three crewmen died because of this vicious attack. The 500 pound bomb penetrated the St.Lo's flight deck and started a huge gasoline fire. The enormous fire spread and actually got inside the St.Lo's torpedo and bomb magazine. There were altogether six huge explosions.

There were 889 men originally aboard the St.Lo. Four ships came to her rescue. The U.S.S. Dennis picked up 434 members of the St.Lo's crew. The U.S.S. Raymond, U.S.S. Heermann and the U.S.S. John C. Butler picked up the rest out of the Pacific Ocean's salt water. It only took less than thirty minutes for the St.Lo to sink. Ed told me she was listing and sinking quickly from the six massive explosives.

The small American escort carrier group, called Taffy 3, fought valiantly. They did some damage to the much larger Japanese fleet. The Americans lost the U.S.S. St.Lo, the U.S.S. Gambier Bay, the destroyers U.S.S. Johnston and the U.S.S. Hoel, and the destroyer escort U.S.S. Samuel B. Roberts.

The St.Lo received four battle stars for her World War II combat. Ed received the presidential bronze star for his World War II service.

Japanese admiral Kurita broke off the surface battle and withdrew to the San Bernadino Strait on the night of October 25, 1944. Our invasion troops that were battling on Leyte were saved from a Japanese Naval bombardment by the bravery of Ed and the other Naval personnel aboard the ships of Taffy 3.

# Chapter XIX

# The B 17 Sugar Beet Field Belly Landing

## Story of *John E. Phillips*

John Phillips was a tail gunner on an American bomber B 17 during World War II. He was born in Alcorn County near Corinth, MS.

John did his basic training at Keesler Airbase near Biloxi, MS. He passed the pilot training program test. Because they had too many pilots, they gave him three choices: tail gunner, infantry, or airplane mechanic. John picked tail gunner. He did his gunnery training at Kingman, Arizona.

John became a member of the 303 Bomb group, Hells Angels, of the 8th Air Force. He was stationed at Molesworth, England. Each crew would have five combat missions

**John Phillips**
*(Courtesy of John Phillips)*

in a row, and then the crew would receive leave to R&R (rest and relaxation).

On John's 11th mission all "hell broke loose." The date was the 18th of March of 1945. The primary target was the Berlin, Germany,

Railroad Marshalling yards ( train switching and loading yards). Thirty eight B-17's with 179 P-51's, as their escorts, struck the Berlin target. Flak was very intense and John's plane was hit. His engines went out and also the left aileron was out. The plane's gas lines and oil lines were also damaged. The pilot, Captain James Cassels, stabilized the now erratic nose diving of the plane. The brave, young pilot was going to stay with the crippled plane and let John and the crew bail out. Captain James Cassels then announced on the intercom that he would try to make a belly landing at Nasielsk, Poland, which was a bomb damaged runway. It was located 25 miles Northwest of Warsaw, Poland.

On approaching the base, a Russian Yak fighter plane made a pass firing at John's B-17 plane. John Phillip's immediately returned the fire and the Yak finally retreated away. Captain Cassels made a perfect "belly landing" (wheels up) in a sugar beet field next to the Nasielsk bomb damaged runway. No one on board the crippled B-17 was injured or hurt during the emergency landing. Also, the plane did not catch on fire. We can thank God for the "wet sugar beets." The crew was now called "escapees", not captured.

Very young Russians came out in a horse drawn cart and picked all eight crew members up and placed them in a Polish home. They were fed well and they stayed several days. One day, John was even taken to a wedding by the Polish family. After interrogating John about shooting at the Yak, the Russians said that the Yak pilot was "trigger happy." John told him that he had shot at them first and that is why he shot at the S.O.B.

Later on, John said that they took his crew and him to Warsaw. He viewed it as almost completely destroyed much like the Japanese did to Manila. The Russians placed them in a building temporarily with many other nationalities. After a while the crew was placed in a railroad boxcar, a very similar boxcar to the one that was in the movie Dr. Zhivago. It contained a potbellied stove and a "slop" bucket to do your business. A bag of raw potatoes and loaves of black bread were delivered daily for the crew to boil and eat. After two weeks of living in the boxcar, the crew was taken to an American base in Poltava, Russia. From there they were given orders to return to England. For the next 42 days they were traveling back home to Molesworth, England. They traveled by way of Russia, Iran, Greece, Italy, and France. Germany had already surrendered when they arrived in England, although Japan was still fighting the Allies.

**John Phillips**
*(Courtesy of John Phillips)*

**Jack Robinson, 3rd Army Tanker**
*(Courtesy of Eddie Robinson)*

# Chapter XX

# The U.S.S. Neosho, December 7, 1941 U.S. Navy Patrol Squadron VP-63 (MAD-CAT)

## Story of *Howard Lee*

The U.S.S. Neosho, a refueling ship, was sitting peacefully between the battleships California and Oklahoma on December 7, 1941. Howard Lee was getting a ride to San Diego on the Neosho. The trip was for his well deserved shore leave for rest and relaxation. The U.S.S. Argonne, a Navy supply ship, Howard's home was across the harbor, not too far from the U.S.S. Neosho. The U.S.S. Neosho had an enormous amount of fuel aboard.

Petty officer, Howard Lee, witnessed the first bomb

**Howard Lee**
*(Courtesy of Howard Lee)*

from the Japanese planes explode. That particular bomb took out a "plane hanger" on Ford Island, inside Pearl Harbor.

The Neosho was ignored by the greedy Japanese pilots who were only trying to sink the many large U.S. Battleships, Cruisers, and Destroyers. The Neosho eventually backed over to Mary's Point where the U.S. submarines stood moored. The Japanese pilots continued to ignore the Neosho.

Late at night on December 7 five unannounced Navy fighters from the U.S.S. Enterprise aircraft carrier tried to land at the Pearl Harbor air base. Four were immediately shot down and only one was successful in landing. Howard said that the Neosho fueled up the U.S.S. Enterprise in the early a.m. of December 8, 1941, the carrier got out of the harbor before dawn.

Howard's experiences at Pearl Harbor, aboard the Neosho, are without comparison to any that I have ever heard. The Neosho was sunk in 1942 at The Battle of the Coral Sea. The Neosho was originally given to the U.S. Navy before World War II by the Esso Oil Company.

Howard Lee is originally from Crawfordsville, Indiana. He retired from the Navy on June 30, 1960. Howard worked as a stock broker in Memphis, TN for 42 years. He retired in the year of 2002. His late wife's name was Kay. Today, Howard resides in Memphis, TN and still enjoys his family and friends.

## *U.S. Navy Patrol Squadron VP-63 (MAD-CAT)*

Howard Lee said Columbia University developed the Magnetic Anomaly Detector (MAD) system for the Navy. It would let the Navy PBY-5 (sea plane) fly over a German U-Boat and magnetically locate its position.

Scientists at the California Institute of technology developed a retro firing rocket bomb for destroying U-Boats. Twelve sixty pound bombs were attached under each wing of the PBY-5s. The retro firing rocket would fire forward killing the speed of the plane, causing the bombs to fall with no forward trajectory. The bombs were fired in intervals. Only one plane at a time would make a bombing attack.

Howard Lee's Naval Patrol Squadron VP-63 (MAD-CAT) worked the straits of Gibraltar. They were given the location of all known sunken ships. The "magnetic needle" (MAD-CAT) could not distinguish between a U-Boat and sunken ship. It would swing for a sunken ship.

On February 8, 1944, a magnetic fence patrol began between the Spanish side and the Spanish Morocco side of the straits of Gibraltor. The PBY Navy patrol Squadron,VP-63, planes covered the fence by flying two planes 180 degrees apart from dawn to dusk. The invasion of South France was coming and the U-Boats entering the Mediterranean were targeted.

Two of the VP-63 "MAD-CATS" flying the magnetic fence on February 24, 1944 followed and tracked German U-Boat 761. An attack was made and the German subs commander had to surface because of severe damage. A nearby British destroyer arrived and picked up the German crew. The German U-Boat captain could not understand that "no surface ships sank his U-Boat." The bombs had contact fuses and would not explode unless they hit something.

On March 16, 1944 U-Boat 392 was sunk and on April 15, 1944 U-Boat 731 was sent to the bottom. The German naval high commander said on May 20, 1944 that no more U-Boats were to enter the Mediterranean Sea. They explained that this was because of excessive losses in the straits of Gibraltar.

Howard Lee quoted from his "MAD-CAT" skipper captain, Eddie Wagner: "The difficult we do immediately, the impossible takes a little longer." Howard Lee was still a dedicated "MAD-CAT" when I interviewed him at his "Pent House" home on July 2, 2008.

**Kay and Howard Lee**
*(Courtesy of Howard Lee)*

# Chapter XXI

# Memphis Memories and My Observations

## Stories by *Victor L. Robilio Jr.*

Growing up in Memphis, TN during World War II was a unique experience. I was six when World War II ended. We had a lot of excitement!

My mom and dad (Cecilia and Victor L. Robilio) had a Navy pilot and his wife stay in our home while the U.S. government rushed to finish Millington, TN's naval air station. Millington was located just a few miles North of Memphis. It was a new and large naval air and technical training command base.

The radio message of the Japanese sneak attack at Pearl Harbor received on Sunday morning, December 7, 1941, upset my family and me. I heard it with my dad while my mom was at St.Theresa Catholic Church attending services. Four of my dad's brothers telephoned and told him that they were going to volunteer. Three went into the regular Army and one joined the Air Corp. My dad said that he was joining company B, "I will B here when you leave and I will B here when you get back." He was too old. All were sons of an Italian immigrant named John S. Robilio. He was also my grandfather!

We had the same old car, a blue Chevy, for the duration of the war. During this time of war they were not making any new civilian vehicles, also gas was rationed and tires were very scarce. My mom called her Chevy "old blue eyes." Her brakes were not very good and she almost ran into the Mississippi River on two different occasions. I remember the high water churning along the side of Riverside Park's muddy and steep banks as mom struggled with "old blue eye's" two sets of brakes. The other brake problem was on Union Avenue near Front Street. This took place on a very steep Memphis bluff. As we rolled toward the Mississippi River, mom's brakes gave out and panic set in. Finally, her emergency brake kicked in and held.

Japanese mini-submarines came up the Mississippi River from New Orleans past Memphis to spy. They got all the way to St.Louis, Missouri before they were discovered and disposed of by the United States Coast Guard.

Most children, like me, who were exposed to the news, had very imaginative dreams during the night. I had dreams that the Nazi's were going to get me and put me in one of their concentration camps. I also dreamed that the Japanese were going to capture me and take me back to Japan.

One afternoon my mom and dad took me to my Grandmother's house which was located on South McNeil Street in Memphis, TN. When we crossed over North Parkway (near Snowden School) we viewed a plane that was flying very low, right over the tops of the trees. There were some young men standing in the doorways of the plane. When we arrived at my Grandmother's house she ran outside and about that time there was a very large sound, such as two trains colliding. It scared Grandmother and me so bad that we both began to cry. The plane that we had seen on North Parkway had crashed and took out three houses on Garland Street; five people were killed during this incident (two in the houses and three in the plane). I personally think that the plane was lost and had run out of fuel. The next day some local children brought me a souvenir from inside of the plane. It was a cockpit control panel part.

Going to church during World War II was a unique experience. Monsignor Whitfield founded St. Theresa Catholic Church, in North Memphis, in the 1930's. He insisted that we sing "Praise the Lord and Pass the Ammunition" at all services during World War II. I was an altar boy after the war. He would say to me, "Mulligan, pour all of the wine into the chalice". He was very stern and we all jumped at his commands.

After World War II Father Vincent Hines arrived to assist Monsignor Whitfield. He was much like Bing Crosby in "Bells of St. Mary's". Father Hines was on a "search and rescue" Navy BPY during the war. He was very handsome, kind, gentle, and an inspiration to all us young people. Father Hines had a scar down one side of his face from a Navy PBY "search and rescue" accident. I was able to play golf with Father Vincent Hines one day at Overton Golf Course in Mid-town, Memphis. He could drive the ball 250 yards. He was truly an inspiration to all.

## *My Observations:*

Wealth has turned into "Wall Street Greed" in today's business climate. It is not "In God We Trust" like it was during World War II. The greedy Wall Street type, business executives believe, "In Wealth and Greed we Trust". The true gentle God, who helped us defeat the Godless fascist of Nazi Germany and the cruel and bestial Japanese military, is being ignored. The new wealth (god) is worshiped with how much money you possess, how many "trophy" wives you have had, how much you can underpay your loyal employees, and how little charitable donations you give to your church or various charities. This was not the way that it was during World War II!

During World War II the chaplains were respected and revered. Sergeant Tom McCarthy told us of going to mass, held on top of a 3rd Army jeep, right before the "Battle of the Bulge". Casualties were enormous in his division.

The Roosevelt and Truman presidencies made the U.S.A. "Leader of the World". Let's reinvent ourselves and cast out the "wealth god" and replace it with the true God of our Fathers.

I firmly believe the current wave of Latino immigrants will refocus us from selfishness and arrogance to humility. The "hate mongers" among us who are against immigration are truly sick people. They are the same type of people that enabled the Jewish people and civilian justice to be decimated in Europe.

My grandfather emigrated from the Po River Valley of Northern Italy in 1901. I was named after the Italian King Victor Emmanuel II, who united all of Italy during the 1870's. During World War II sons of German, French, Spanish, Scottish, English, Italian, Greek, and Polish immigrants smashed and decimated the Nazi war machine. I have talked to, interviewed, recorded, and video taped over 200 of them. They were all truly citizen soldiers and our heroes. May God bless them all!

**Jennie and John S. Robilio**
**Victor Robilio's Grandparents**
*(Courtesy of Victor L. Robilio Jr)*

# Chapter XXII

# The Naval Air Combat Intelligence Officer

## Story of *Charles M. Crump*

Charles finished law school in 1937. He took a tour of Europe during the summer of 1937. He made a picture of Hitler standing on the second floor balcony of a hotel. This chance tourist viewing of Hitler took place in Nuremburg. Charles viewed Germany before its destruction but he knew the prospect of war was inevitable.

Charles was married in July of 1940 and his son Met was born in 1942, his son Philip was born in 1944, and his son Stephen was born in 1948. In January of 1939 he became a member of the Tennessee Legislature and served two terms of two years each.

Charles volunteered for the Navy in February 1943. Because of his poor eye sight, the Navy said that Charles was physically unacceptable. This did not discourage Charles. He went five days a week, from August 1943 to December 1943, for eye exercises. He finally got a physically acceptable letter from the Navy, and was commissioned a naval officer in November of 1943.

Charles was sent to Quonset Point, Rhode Island in January of 1944 for training. He said the Navy gave "Billet Interviews" when a person was changing positions. Charles heard of an A.C.I. (Air Combat Intelligence) position. He fortunately got the position in the Navy A.C.I. Charles duties included briefing the pilots before they left on missions. Then, he would interrogate the pilots on return and write up a Navy Air Combat report.

The dive bombing planes used by the Navy Aircraft carriers in 1944 and in 1945 were the SB2C Hell Diver (Curtiss Wright produced.) It was designated the Scout Bomber 2nd Curtiss.

Charles was assigned to a new carrier called the Shangri-La (CV-38). It was named after a mythical kingdom described in the book, "Lost Horizon", by James Hilton.

He had been taught how to recognize ships and planes of the Axis and the Allies and he had taught this skill to the pilots and air crewmen of Dive Bombing Squadron VB-85. The Navy used cards and silhouettes that were from all different views and angels. The images would stay in one's mind (American, Japanese, German, etc.)

In January 1945 the Shangri-La sailed for San Diego through the Panama Canal. On arrival, they were told the crew was too slow in getting planes off the deck for combat. The Shangri-La was then sent to the Hawaiian Islands for deck crew training and the airgroup was sent to Maui. The Shangri-La CV-38 spent two months there while the crew practiced to become faster. Charles told me that the U.S.S. Aircraft Carrier Franklin docked next to the Shangri-La at Pearl Harbor. He could see a big hole clear through the flight deck. Japanese kamikazes had really pounded the Franklin off Japan. She was a brand new carrier when she arrived there. The attack killed all the pilots in the ready room under the hanger deck's 3 inch cover of steel. The crew opened the room door and found them all dead from concussion of 600 pound kamikaze bombs.

Charles also said he viewed black smoke coming from a U.S.S. Aircraft carrier; it was the Hornet, which was in Shangri-La's quadrant at the battle of Okinawa. The other carrier, like the Franklin, was hit by Kamikazes. She did not sink but many were killed by the Japanese.

Charles said that the Shangri-La arrived at Okinawa on April 25, of 1945. On arrival she pounded the Japanese close in support of American ground troops.

After Okinawa was secured, the American task force, including the Shangri-La, attacked the Japanese home islands until mid-August.

President Harry Truman dropped two atomic bombs on Japan on August 6th and 9th, 1945 which caused them to surrender on August 15, 1945. They did not know we only had two atomic bombs. Harry Truman was not about to tell them. They signed the surrender document in Tokyo Harbor on September 2, 1945. The war would have gone on indefinitely with huge casualties on both sides had the atomic bombs not been dropped.

The Shangri-La returned to San Diego and was greeted by a large sign on a harbor warehouse which read "Well Done, Welcome Home!" Charles was sent to Philadelphia as a "Naval Contract Termination Officer". The Navy was going to a Peace Time "Logistics Posture" as quickly as possible, and after a few months, Charles was discharged to return to civilian life.

*(Courtesy of Charles Crump)*

**Charles Crump
in his 20's**
*(Courtesy of Met Crump)*

**Charles Crump, taken in 2003, when he was 90**
*(Courtesy of Met Crump)*

**Aircraft Action Report**
*(Courtesy of Charles Crump)*

# Chapter XXIII

# C47 Pilot at the Battle of Manila

## Story of *Frank Moynahan*

Frank got out of flight school in August 1944. He was first stationed in Biak, New Guinea and then was moved and re-stationed near Manila on Luzon Island. He was in the Philippines during the vicious battle for Manila. Frank brought supplies in and flew the wounded out to his base on Luzon. A hospital was located there to treat the American G.I.'s that had been wounded. He landed on the

**Frank Moynahan (2nd from left)**
*(Courtesy of Frank Moynahan)*

famous Manila Road called "Quezon City Blvd." It was the main street of Manila during the battle for Manila. All light and telephone polls were leveled by bulldozers. Also, battle debris was pushed out of the way. The Japanese made a stand in the "old city" near the harbor. They caused the city to be devastated, much like Warsaw, Poland and Berlin, Germany.

A C47 had two pilots, plus an engineer, and a radio operator. Frank said that they lost one plane out of his squadron and its crew in the Philippines operation. Over 100,000 Philippines civilians were killed during the Battle of Manila. 16,000 Japanese Army, Marine, and Navy personnel were also killed. 1,000 American soldiers died and 5,500 were wounded. A Japanese Admiral would not make Manila an "open city" like McArthur had done in 1942. In the annuals of history, the bestial attitude of the Japanese at Manila and in the Philippines should never be forgotten. Innocent civilians were tortured, raped, and murdered by the vicious Japanese Marines.

After the Battle of Manila, Frank was sent to supply U.S. Army troops battling the Japanese on the North end of Luzon Island. He had to land on ultra short jungle airstrips. Japanese jungle snipers shot at him when he landed and took off. His plane was riddled and shot up but not a single crew member was injured.

Frank's unit was then ordered to IeShima Island next to Okinawa. This was toward the close of the war. He viewed 1,300 ships and boats in the Okinawa area. Included in those numbers were eighteen battleships and fourteen cruisers.

The dropping of the atomic bombs on Japan ended the war. Frank was on Okinawa when the bombs were dropped. The N.C.O.'s predicted 60% to 70% casualties during an invasion of Japan. The two bombs actually saved lives. The Japanese would never surrender. Their casualties could have reached 3 million with the United States possibly taking 1,000,000 casualties.

After the surrender, Frank flew to Tokyo, Japan to pick up American P.O.W.s'. He was greeted like a diplomat by the Japanese. The P.O.W.'s were in terrible shape. They were in various camps around Japan. He said they were very malnourished and weak. The Japanese had treated them inhumanely. Frank flew them to Tokyo for rehabilitation and shipment home.

In 2006, after fifty years of flying, Frank was awarded the FAA's coveted Wright Brothers Master Pilot Award. During his flying experiences he had two close calls. One was during the Battle of Manila, where he was allowed to fly a P51 fighter plane. When Frank took off from the base he had carburetor problems and had to return immediately to the runway. The second close call is a rather humorous story. Frank was flying along Interstate 75 in Florida. Frank's plane ran out of oil and he had to land immediately in between two Interstate 75 roads on the grass median strip. Frank just happened to land near a Hooter's Restaurant. With cooperation of the Highway patrol the female waitresses were allowed to pose for a picture with Frank in front of the airplane (which was near Hooters). Hooter's new billboard read as follow: "Hooters- now offering fly through service." This story hit the U.S.A. wire services and newspapers world wide.

Frank is now retired and currently lives in Newnan, Georgia. I am sorry to report his wife passed recently.

**Conference —**
**Jap. Envoys to disarm Japan and return P.O.W.'s**
*(Courtesy of Frank Moynahan)*

# Chapter XXIV

# The Brave C47 Combat Pilot of the Burma, China, and India Theatres

## Story of *George Livers*

The C47 was a "work horse" supply plane that was used during World War II. It was called "Ol Dumbo" by the troops. The Allies used it to carry troops, supplies, and pack animals. The British called it "Dakota" and we called it a DC3 (civilian plane) or a C47 (Army Air Corp plane) It helped win the war.

George Livers was stationed in India near the border with Burma. The Japanese were pounding and pushing the combined: Chinese, American, Australian, British, and Indian troops completely out of Burma. George flew supplies to them often and sadly watched them lose practically all of Burma to the Japanese.

One day he delivered some machine guns and ammunition to the Allies. He spoke to the wasted looking and exhausted British troops and said that he could easily fly them back to India. They said, "No, do not worry, we will walk out. Then, they said, "When we reach the Indian border we will turn and pound the Japanese. They said, "the Gurkha Indian troops, from Nepal, will parachute in and cut off both their heads and their supply lines." A while later this is exactly what happened.

George was returning from Kunming, China one night and set a C47 altitude record of 19,000 feet. He was lost that evening for a while in the Himalayas. A vigilant Army short wave radio operator guided him back to his air base in Assam, India.

On one Burma flight George picked up a wounded British doctor after a battle with the Japanese. The doctor had to amputate his own leg. He was remarkably in good spirits and excellent health. He chatted with George.

After the battle for Myitkyina, Burma , Merrill's Marauder's were given leave. They had captured the airfield but not the city. The Japanese eventually recaptured the airfield which upset Merrill. He went to the hospital and talked to his lightly wounded Marauders. They told him that they would go back and retake the airfield plus the city. George said that Merrill's Marauders ran the Japanese out of the airfield and city. What courage!

During the attack on Southern Indian cities, the Japanese Burma Army was defeated because they brought no food supplies. They had to retreat with no food. The Allies made sure no supplies could be found along the Burma- India border. They mistakenly thought they could live off the land!

George Livers told me two humorous stories about flying mules and goats. The American troops in Burma needed Tennessee red mules to move artillery over mountains. George said the Tennessee mules were "quiet messy" and the entire plane cargo area had to be scrubbed down and fumigated after their delivery. He said that they did not like the air trip at all.

Some British and Australian troops in Burma wanted milk and mutton. George was asked if he would deliver them some goats. The pilot entrance to a C47 is through the cargo area. George had a big mess to smell and walk through. Most supplies were loaded aboard his C47 plane at 12:00 midnight with George and his crew arriving around 6:00 a.m. After a short delivery flight to the British unit, he found them very appreciative.

Then, he was asked to deliver needed oil to another British unit field kitchen without cleaning up the plane after the goats. The cooking oil then leaked, on take off, into the goat mess. Without cleaning up, the next flight was an emergency flight for Chinese nationalists' troops and dependents needed in China. They were wanted immediately because the Japanese had broken through the main Chinese defense line. They "all smiled" at George when they were boarding the plane but soon became very sick to their stomachs during the entire flight.

George told me the C47 could fly just about anything anywhere as long as you clean it up after each flight. He said the delivery of the goats, cooking oil, Chinese nationalist's troops, and dependents was very challenging to say the least.

We are sorry that George passed on June 19, 2012 in Memphis, TN.


## *Journal by George Livers*

**Colonel George M. Livers**
**United States Air Force**

My military career began in October 1941 in Martinsburg, West Virginia. I enlisted in the Army Air Corp. as a "buck" private with pay of $21.00 a month. I arrived at Kessler Army Base in Mississippi where I was stationed for several months. I received my orders to pilot school and was assigned to Maxwell AAFB, concluding my pilot training and received my coveted "Silver Pilot Wing" at Valdosta AAFB, Georgia, in December 1942.

My first assignment was to the Military Transport Command at Memphis, Tennessee, assigned to deliver all types of aircraft- fighters, transports and bombers- within the continental United States, as well as overseas. I was assigned to overseas delivery with flights to North Africa, England and India. I was sub-sequentially assigned to the 4th Combat Cargo Group, forming at Morrison Field, Miami, Florida. The Group was made up of 100 new C-47 aircraft and involved four squadrons of 25 aircraft each. We knew that we were headed for England for the anticipated European landing . As it turned out we were opening our orders after take off, and climbing over Miami Beach and to my surprise our orders for our final destination was India.

My first mission upon arriving in India was to deliver supplies of all types to a British base. We found the small airstrip and on final approach received small arms fire from the Japanese force hiding in the hills surrounding the area. Upon landing safely we loaded wounded and dead for a quick departure. We offered to move troops back to India, but the "Jolly" British troopers said that they would walk out and see us in India.

General "Vinegar Joe" Stillwell did walk out of Burma with the remaining British and Indian troops, the Japs having taken control of the Burma Road, the last land line to China. General Stillwell moved north to the Assam Valley of India. Here he formed a new force, building a new road to China called the Ledo Road. Our squadrons also moved north with a mission to support General Stillwell. We flew everything, from food to ammunition, water, and all of the equipment needed to build the new roadway through the jungle. One mission involved a load of Tennessee red full size mules, all well received by the troops and were needed to assist in moving guns, carts, and pulling trucks out of mud.

Another mission involved a load of full grown goats, and had been on the plane since mid-night. They were to be delivered to the British for milk and food. Off loading the goats, we were then asked to deliver cans of cooking oil to a close base. The cans broke open of course, adding to the mess in the cargo area created by the load of goats. We delivered the oil and were told that we were to deliver a load of Chinese troops to Kunming China, as directed by General Chiang Kai-Shek. I never knew how many Chinese troops were on board my flight, but as I entered the aircraft they were all smiling. The troops also carried all types of equipment, including a "kitchen sink" and a few females. Having never flown the Himalayas we fortunately had good clear weather and found a pass, headed east for Kunming. One thing about the Chinese, they see an aircraft and immediately get sick. This was so true, with all throwing-up, which added to our mess by the goats, the broken cooking oil and now the load of Chinese. Needless to say, I was not the most popular aircraft commander upon arrival at my home base.

Other missions involved supporting General Merrell's Mauraders in defeating the Japs at Mitchenau, the base city of the Burma Road. One other mission called for supplies to a British camp that had been hit by the Japs overnight. We loaded the wounded and others. One was their British doctor who had been severely wounded and in fact had cut off his own leg to save his life. He appeared fairly jolly, in the usual British manner, and we delivered our wounded to the Ledo hospital in northern India.

Having completed one year in the China Burma India Combat Area with 1,000 combat flying hours and being promoted to Captain, I received orders to the good old U S of A.

After numerous very active and interesting assignments, my final retirement, October 1971, as Base Commader of Pope Air Force Base, N.C., brought about the end of my great 30 year Air Force Career.

**1929 – Cecilia Robilio and Halbert Knox
USMC (Pearl Harbor)**
*(Courtesy of Victor L. Robilio Jr.)*

# CHAPTER XXV

# ARUBA, U-BOATS

## Story of *Lenoir Black*

In High School Lenoir had passed the V-12 program in the eleventh grade. It was for "officer's candidate school." He did not attend.

Lenoir enlisted in the Navy in 1944. He went to Great Lakes boot camp in the Chicago area. Lenoir also went to St.Louis University to a special school about underwater direct currents. He graduated from submarine school in New London, Connecticut.

**Lenoir Black, 1944**
*(Courtesy of Lenoir Black)*

Lenoir was assigned to boat #214, The USS Grouper, in February of 1945. He was an enlisted sailor.

The Grouper was sent to destroy die hard U-Boat operations near Aruba in the Caribbean area. The U-Boats worked in Wolf packs. They attacked oil tankers leaving the Harbor of the island of Aruba. This was in February and March of 1945. Some of these U-Boat captains would not surrender in May of 1945 when Germany surrendered.

Aruba was only ninety miles from Venezuela. Fruit juices, oranges, and other supplies were picked up by the U.S.S. Grouper from friendly nearby islands.

Submarines were called boats not ships. The Grouper sunk two U-Boats but only got credit for sinking one. Lenoir had a ninety day tour of combat duty. Between eighteen and twenty oil tankers would leave Aruba in a convoy bound for U.S. refineries, they were sitting ducks. Destroyers and cruisers would escort them through the Wolf-Pack infested waters. Sonar picked up the U-Boats positions.

The scariest thing on Lenoir's tour of duty was when a U-Boat unintentionally resurfaced under the USS Grouper and made a cross with the two boats. The U-Boat almost hit the U.S.S. Grouper. It was a close call.

Lenoir visited captured German U-Boats and said that they were very clean. They also had elaborate oak paneling. He met U-Boat prisoners and said they looked "wasted and worn out." Lenoir also visited a British boat but said it had a bad odor and was not up to the U.S. and German's quality standards of workmanship.

**Lenoir Black, 1944**
*(Courtesy of Lenoir Black)*

# CHAPTER XXVI

# RIVALS: FIRST MATE DAVID CONWELL AND ADMIRAL KARL DOENITZ

## by *John R. S. Robilio*

Hardly a cloud blemished the mid-day sun as the Alcoa Puritan ploughed steadily through the Gulf of Mexico on May 6th, 1942. Laden with bauxite, she had traversed all but 100 miles of her journey from Trinidad to Mobile. The temperature hovered at a pleasant 80 degrees. Everything appeared peaceful.

First Mate David Conwell checked his watch and delighted in the realization that only thirty minutes separated him from lunch. Today, lunch would be special insofar as fried chicken, turnip greens and corn bread punctuated the menu. These items especially stimulated his appetite and he relished his imminent visit to the officers' Mess room. He would consume his meal with alacrity. Moreover, he and his crew would be afforded the amenities of Mobile within twenty-four hours. The notion of rest and recreation pleased everyone.

Kapitanleutnant Harro Schacht, the battle-hardened commander of U-507, entertained different plans for Conwell and his shipmates. Schacht had stalked the Alcoa Puritan for over an hour assuring himself that no aircraft or warships protected her. The Alcoa Puritan, he concluded, sailed alone and he would assault her.

His first torpedo barely missed the starboard bow and thereafter, Conwell and his men scrambled to their battle stations. U-507 surfaced at about 11:35 a.m. and Schacht directed his men to their

4.1 inch deck gun. According to Conwell the shelling lasted about twenty to thirty minutes and resulted in very substantial damage to the Alcoa Puritan. Miraculously, no crew members were killed though a few sustained injuries. Conwell complied with his captain's order to abandon ship and all crew members were evacuated safely into lifeboats. As Conwell proceeded away from his dying ship he observed Kapitanleutnant Schacht on the conning tower of U-507. In knightly fashion Schacht uttered to Conwell and his terrified shipmates "I do hope you get back safely. I am sorry that I had to do it." For Conwell and his crew safety would come in the form of the Coast Guard cutter Boutwell. She would retrieve them from the perils of the open sea and would deposit them at Morgan City, Louisiana. "Land never looked so beautiful," remarked Conwell.

Another ship had been consigned to the ever-growing list of allied obituaries. Admiral Karl Doenitz, Germany's consummate strategist and the master brain behind submarine warfare, had snatched another victim. Bauxite, the principal component of aluminum, and thus the framework of airplanes, had been denied the battered British and Soviets. Regrettably, by the end of summer 1942, many allied ships would litter the bottom of the Gulf of Mexico.

For the allies and First Mate David Conwell, Doenitz represented a formidable adversary. Doenitz had served with distinction as a submariner in World War I and had pioneered the tactic of night surface attacks. He had declared that Germany had underestimated the potential of submarine warfare in the Great War and he had boasted that the submarine possessed the potential of delivering death blows to the allies in the Second World War. He contended that the production and deployment of 300 U-boats would symbolize the destruction of allied power. An ardent Nazi he had praised Adolf Hitler commenting that "he would save Germany from the disintegrating poison of World Jewry." In fact, Doenitz would succeed Hitler and would rule Germany for a matter of weeks before his arrest.

During the thirties Germany had defied the provisions of the Versailles Treat and had commenced the task of rebuilding her navy. The construction of fearsome battleships like the Bismarck and the Tirpitz coupled with awesome cruisers in the form of the Scharnhorst and the Gneisenau engendered little enthusiasm from Doenitz. The submarine and the airplanes, argued Doenitz, would tip the scale. Large capital ships would no longer dominate the seven seas. They would not escape aircraft and submarines and they would suffer large losses.

Hitler admired the loyalty and enterprise of Doenitz but he demonstrated only a very small measure of interest in naval matters. Hitler envisioned global victory in terms of colossal land battles that would vanquish the foes of the Third Reich and would establish Germany as the preponderant power on this planet. Frequently, Doenitz denounced harshly the blindness of the Nazi regime for not developing naval air power. Fortunately, for the sake of humanity, Hitler did not understand fully sea power.

In combating the allies Doenitz created new concepts of naval warfare. He stressed the importance of avoiding confrontations with the Leviathans of the Royal Navy but he counseled his officers to assault mercilessly the numerous merchant ships that fed and armed the British and their far-flung allies. By puncturing at various sensitive points the lengthy, convoluted arteries of supply that connected the widely dispersed allies a massive, irreparable hemorrhage might ensue. Such a catastrophe might occasion peace overtures from the allied camp. Smashing the shipping routes of the allies might denote victory for Germany.

Doenitz contended that Germany could achieve victory by the deployment of three hundred U-boats against the allies. Severing the supply arteries of the allies would bring about peace moves and would nullify the might of the Royal Navy. Doenitz did not realize his objective of piercing the allied supply arteries and a collapse in the allied war efforts. Comprehensive air cover linked with armed convoys would signal devastation for the German U-boat force by the end of May 1943. However, Doenitz would come dangerously close to halting the flow of allied supplies in the winter of 1940 and 1941 and the first six months of 1942. From September 1, 1939 to May 8, 1945 the efforts of Karl Doenitz resulted in the sinking of 2,900 allied vessels and the death of 30,248 allied sailors.

Doenitz would accept egregious losses: 783 submarines, 28,000 sailors and the Battle of the Atlantic. First Mate David Conwell and the allies would triumph.

**John R. S. Robilio**
*(Courtesy of Victor L. Robilio Jr.)*

# Chapter XXVII

# The First 10 Howitzers to Cross the Rhine River

## Story of *John Meihofer*

John Meihofer volunteered on June 20, 1942 to join the United States Army. He was from St. Louis, Missouri. John was trained at Camp Hood in the state of Texas. He was assigned to the tank destroyer school. John spoke fluent German.

Later on, John was shipped to Scotland on a small cruise ship. John's brother, Elmer Meihofer Jr., and he fought as part of George Patton's 3rd Army.

His father, Elmer Meihofer (was assigned to Houston Anti Air Defense), trained Army troops in Texas during the war.

John was assigned to the 241st Field Artillery Batallion of the 3rd Army.

**John Meihofer (right) and Elmer Jr. meet on German bridge.**
*(Courtesy of John Meihofer)*

He was with the first ten 105 Howitzers to cross the Rhine River into Germany. We supported the 51st Armored Infantry many times and sent word back and forth. His brother, Elmer, appeared and surprised him one day while he was standing on a bridge inside Germany. They had been separated during the many 3rd Army battles against the Germans. Both met again, at the war's end, at Linz, Austria.

John was among some of the first American soldiers to liberate Dachau Concentration Camp. The camp was near the town of Zorneding, Germany. The Germans had set up "bone crushers" and "meat grinders" inside some of the rooms. Beside one Dachau building was a bloody ditch. John also observed a huge mass grave. He made many pictures with his brownie camera. After the war, John helped displaced persons get back home by escorting them. He and General Eisenhower knew that the beastly things that they saw would be denied within fifty years after the war. Eisenhower made many pictures to destroy any lying by the perpetrators today. We are experiencing denials today by some of the uneducated radicals and would be terrorists.

John has been back to visit Dachau, once with his wife, Betty Jean, and once with his son. The German female tour guide said that the "showers" at Dachau were for "water baths", not poison gas. John asked her where the "bone crushers" and "meat grinders" were. They had been removed and were no where to be seen. She did not answer him. This proves the cover up that he and General Eisenhower had predicted in 1945. There are no tour guides today at Dachau.

The crimes against humanity that were perpetuated by Adolph Hitler and his followers should always be remembered. The

**Mr. and Mrs. John Meihofer**
*(Courtesy of John Meihofer)*

denial by some people is cause for "concern and vigilance" by us and by all of our allies. The truth should be taught to all of the school children around in the world.

# CHAPTER XXVIII

# MY EXPERIENCES IN WORLD WAR II AS I REMEMBER IT

## Chronological Excerpts from a Journal by *Joe E. Warren*

I was inducted into the military service at Camp Robinson at Little Rock, Arkansas on July 21, 1942. I was assigned to the Signal Corps. and was transferred to Camp Crowder in Neosho, Missouri, which was south of Joplin, to receive my basic training. I was at Camp Crowder for four weeks of basic training and was then assigned to Port Arthur, Texas. A group of us boarded the train for Port Arthur, Texas, all assigned to Port Arthur College. We were to be trained to be high speed operators of International Morse Code. We were to learn the code and how to take it on the mill (typewriter). After graduation from college, we received our rating of Technician: Third grade- T/5. I appreciated this rating as my income was very low at this time in my life.

It was near the end of December 1942, when we were issued our impregnated uniforms. We were preparing to go aboard a ship. We were told we were to board the Queen Elizabeth which was 85,000 tons, it was the largest liner ever built at that time. There were about 20,000 other troops that were to cross the Atlantic Ocean in about four days (unescorted) on the Queen Elizabeth. England had been at war for some time and there were shortages that occurred and sacrifices that had to be made. The tea and crumpets (cookies) had no sugar, but I ate and drank them as if they were good. It was early January 1943 when we arrived in England.

In the early part of May 1944, our company was moved to a staging area along with other troops. After we were in the area for a couple of weeks, the Radio Intercept section of the 3250th was moved through Weymouth, England to Portland harbor. We were placed aboard the Ancon. The Ancon was the Command Ship for the Amphibious Fleet. We were aboard the Ancon for ten days before we left the Portland harbor, England. The majority of the equipment of the 3250th Signal Service Company's Radio Intercept section was on the ships that were carrying the other troops to Omaha Beach. The Ancon left Portland Harbor at 2:30 in the afternoon on June 5, 1944 and sailed out to the ocean. We were on our way! It seemed to me that we were leaving early for the invasion to take place on June 6th, but I am sure it took this much time in order for a mission of this size to take place.

The first assault on the beach took place at 6:05 in the morning on June 6th. We knew that the frogmen, engineers and others such as the paratroopers, rangers had all made a lot of progress in their assignments before the assault on the beach again. The 3250th Radio Intercept was asked to go to the Radio section of the ship on the morning of June 6th. Capt. Brownfield assigned frequencies that would be used by the troops on the beach to check to see if we could receive any information about what was happening. We knew that our troops were not too far in, since we had difficulty in securing Omaha Beach. On D + 1, small crafts would come and go from the Ancon. A Higgins boat carried about fifty troops. My first thought was to get some of the weight off, so the Higgins boat would rise when a big wave came. I dropped my pack overboard, making sure that it would land in the bobbing boat. I strapped my Carbine on my back and started down the side of the boat. It did not take long to get ashore because we were only a mile or two off shore. The boat that brought us ashore did a good job; I only had to wade in the water up to my ankles. As we reached the Omaha Beach we could see the destruction of the German bunkers knocked out, and there were underwater obstacles that had been removed. The mine fields were marked off with stakes and ribbon. You could hear plenty of firing from the Navy as well as from the guns on shore. I knew that our front line troops could not be too far inland, as we could hear their machine-gun fire.

We were told to take off our stripes and insignias as a sniper would kill an officer or non-com first. The Radio Intercept, Direction Finders, the Traffic Analyst section and all of our other facets of our company were ready to be put into action. After all, this was what we had spent the time preparing. We moved gradually inland as the front line progressed. There were many casualties as the troops moved further inland. The front line moved slowly because there were so many casualties in the front line. I remember seeing a six by six truck with dead bodies to be taken back from the front. It was real hard to forget seeing something like that. As the 3250th was progressing forward we reached a place near Belroy near Caumont. The 3250th received a pretty good shelling from the Germans while we were there. The Intercept section was working on receiving German radio transmissions. We could not hear much of what was going on outside. Someone looked out and there was not a soul in sight and then he hollered out, "fellows its coming in". We all threw our headphones off and headed for our foxholes until it was over.

After the break out from the beachhead, we moved further through the hedge rows and apple trees until we reached the city of Vire and on to Flers. Vire was totally destroyed. From Flers we moved to the Chartes area. I know that things were moving so fast that we almost ran through our own lines, but we were stopped by some American troops that told us if we kept going we would be behind the German lines. We retreated. I seem to remember a town in this area called Palaiseou. After we had settled down in the Paris area, we were able to get downtown on several occasions as Paris had been declared an open city. We then moved north and east toward Charleville, in the Mezieres area of France. We crossed the Muese River here in this area. We then moved on to the country of Luxembourg. We then moved to Belgium, arriving at Bastogne in the latter part of October. We remained in Bastogne for some time and moved on to the Houfalize area. The 3250th moved north to St. Vith, Malmedy and then to Eupen in the Belgium area which happened to be four miles from the German border. We arrived in Eupen in late November or early December of 1944. We saw our first buzz bombs flying over in this area. Eupen was a nice area, but the weather was very bad and cold most of the time we were there.

I was granted a three day pass in the early part of December to the rest area in Eupen, Belgium. Marlena Dietrich was in Eupen at this time. While I was on my three day pass, I noticed the large number of tanks and artillery moving south along the highway. I found out that the Germans had launched a major counter attack through the Ardennes. This was the most unlikely place that you would suspect. We were told that the Germans were dropping paratroopers behind the lines that were dressed in American uniforms. I thought that I was lucky for I drew out an assignment to help guard the Command Post in Eupen. I was not so lucky as the Germans came over at night and bombed the railroad yards in Eupen not far from where we were located. I could hardly believe the amount of equipment that was moving south along the highway through Eupen, it was a solid mass. They were moving to contain the break through which was called the Battle of the Bulge.

The Germans had almost complete radio silence. We were usually at this time of the year thinking about Christmas, but we were not thinking about Christmas this year. As the Battle of the Bulge continued, our company was now located four miles from the German border in Eupen which was south of Aachen and north of Elsenborn to our south. This was on Christmas Eve at about 11:00 p.m. Lt. Price and I were out checking our guard positions, when everything broke loose. I do not remember everything that happened that night, and I did not find out until I returned from the hospital. The medics took the dead and the wounded to the basement of the building that we were using for a headquarters for first aid. We were placed in an ambulance and sent back to the aid station for further examination. I was sent back to a hospital in Leige, Belgium for hospitalization for a wound in my right thigh. My biggest problem was that I could not walk and I had a severe contusion. I was immobilized for about six weeks before I could return to my company. In about six weeks I returned to the 3250th Signal Service Company through the replacement depot, by train through Paris. I finally reached company and they were about thirty five miles further back than when I left. I told the guys that every time I left they lost ground. Our company had two killed on that night and we lost three men on one of our direction finders as well as all of their equipment. The direction finding crew was south of us directly in the path of the breakthrough. Sgt. Kalamaris in radio repair was killed and a guy from the Message Center was also killed. Our first sergeant Sgt. Whisenhunt from Oklahoma lost an eye and received severe damage to his right arm. We never heard from him again after that. The company had five or more killed during the Battle of the Bulge, and there were many wounded, with also some minor injuries.

The one thing I always remember is when I first saw a black soldier riding a tank going to the front with a group of white soldiers. The white and blacks were not integrated until the Battle of the Bulge when black soldiers were placed into white units. President Harry S. Truman later declared by executive order that all units would be integrated.

I was in Europe from January of 1943 until October 18, 1945. I received my honorable discharge from the Army at Camp Shelby, Mississippi on October 18, 1945 as a Tech 3. I have gone through five campaigns and the invasion of France and made it back alive. My campaigns were: bronze arrowhead for Invasion, also Normandy, Northern France, Ardennes, Rhineland Central Europe, received five bronze campaign stars. I left Jackson and was on my way to

Pontotoc County, Mississippi, where I was born on September 24, 1921. I arrived by train in Pontotoc and I went 12 miles to Troy, MS where my mother was located. Mrs. John Elbert Warren, better known as Vaudie. My mother never saw me in uniform as I was never on a state side furlough. I was in Europe for the majority of the time.

The above is an Odyssey, as defined in the dictionary, as a long, wandering journey. I agree with this definition, as I must say it was quite an experience serving in World War II. I guess I could say that I became a man in the US Army. I hope that I served my country well and I thank God that I came back alive. I know that I was affected as well as my fellow troop members by their experiences while they were in the service. It is sad that wars have to happen! I will always remember the guys that were killed in the different outfits I was in and also the others who received permanent wounds that will always be a reminder of the war. I hope that I am a better citizen having served

—Joe Warren, written in December of 1995

*P.S.—Thank you to Joe E Warren's niece, Barbara Smith. She let me use his excellent and accurate journal*

# Chapter XXIX

# The 106 Division, 221st Infantry Regiment, Company 1

## Story of *Jim Muskelley*

Jim joined to the A.S.T.P. (Army Specialist Training Program) at the age of seventeen years old. He began his full service on November 10, on his 18th birthday. Jim was trained at Fort Benning, Georgia.

The 106th Division went to Europe in November of 1944. They sailed to Great Britain on the Aquitania. First, the Division was sent to the city of Cheltenham, England. Then, the 106th Division was shipped to LeHavre, France and then trucked up to the Siegfried Line. They were opposing the German Army.

Two regiments of the 106th Division were put on a "hill line" and one was held in reserve. One December 16, 1944 all hell broke loose. The German Army smashed into the 106th Division and overwhelmed them. This "Battle of the Bulge" would go on for a total of forty days and forty nights. Jim Muskelley found himself right in the middle of the battle. Jim and 10,000 American Army troops found themselves in a German trap, they were surrounded!

The 106th Division officers surrendered after talking to the Germans. Jim was told to destroy his weapons. Jim's regiment was still on the high ground but had no artillery. He said the Germans made them walk several days with only one piece of bread, one piece of cheese, and one cup of coffee. Then, they were put into railroad boxcars built for forty soldiers or eight mules. Sixty-six 106 Division troops were put into one boxcar. They had to take turns sitting down. Jim said that he stayed in the boxcar for three weeks and lost fifty pounds. The British bombed the German rail yard (which Jim was in) and mistakenly killed some of the members of his regiment.

Jim's P.O.W camp was located near Dresden, Germany and was called Stalog 4 B. 40,000 Allied P.O.W.s were held at his camp. While at the camp, Jim became sick and had to see a doctor. One of the German guards told him that if he was not sick when he saw the doctor that he would shoot him.

Later, for a work detail outside the P.O.W. camp, Jim swapped names with a British P.O.W. The unfortunate British soldier that swapped names with him was killed by an allied bomb raid while outside the camp. Jim was supposed to be put in solitary confinement for three weeks for swapping names, but was not punished.

Around May 7, 1945 the P.O.W. guards abruptly left the camp. Jim and other allied P.O.W.s walked back West through the Russian lines and towards the American lines.

He spent the first night in the town of Riese, Germany near the Elbe River. The Russians let Jim and four other P.O.W.s stay at a German doctor's two story house. Late that night, two Russians showed up and wanted a German woman. They busted out a large "bay window" in the doctor's house and upset Jim and the other sleeping Allied P.O.W.s. Jim said that the two drunken Russians then went next door and raped a married German Frau whose husband was away in the German Army. Jim said that he "felt like shooting both of the Russians."

Jim walked from Riese, and then over a bridge and into the American lines. The American bridge guard did not want to let them cross the bridge because they looked wasted and not in uniform. All five of them did eventually cross the bridge. The Americans sent trucks and took them to a camp. Then, the Army C47's flew them back to France.

Jim returned to the United States on a cruise ship that was never finished. It was called the H.T. Mayo.

# Chapter XXX

# The Sunderland Flying Boat

## Journal of *Ivor William Wiles* (*Grandfather of Mark Temme*)

*\*Due to space limitations this is not the entire journal; however, very minimal changes have been made to the journal. The grammar used in this journal has been altered to a minimum.*

The war broke out in September of 1939 and our promise to Dad was to redesign the Wiles Steam Cooker. The Wiles invented the food cookers for the Aussie Army. Ken and Dick concentrated on designing the cooker and I became involved in war munitions by carrying out special electroplating processes for the services (the Wiles were inventor's extraordinaires).

My wife, Margaret, and I were married in May of 1939. Margaret thought that we should start our family;

**Ivor Wiles**
*(Courtesy of Mark Temme)*

therefore, Lancelot Ivor was born in July of 1941. Unfortunately, Margaret's health deteriorated. She kept asking for Lance but

I lied and said that he had a cold. Lance died on September 20, 1941. Margaret, unknowing of Lance's death, died on September 21, 1941. They were buried together at Centennial Park. Before all of the problems with Margaret, my Mother had developed a heart problem(she pined for Dad so badly) and she died on April 27, 1941. With the loss of my Father, Mother, Margaret, and Lance my world had collapsed and I was determined to get away to war. I applied for the Air Force the day after Margaret and Lance's funeral.

A call went out to civilians to hand over firearms. Ken who was looking over my few possessions handed over (with my okay) my very good Browning 226 Rifle (automatic), which I used for rabbit shooting. I loved to take a couple of friends on the motor bike and side car to go shooting in and around second valley and Myponga. There was virtually no armament around to protect Australia from attack. The defensive position was critical.

According to Dr. Hetler, I had failed eyesight which was not suitable for Royal Australian Air Force. My eye strength was unbalanced and it was demanded that I be tested by a specialist by the name of Dr. Tostevin. Dr.Hetler's rooms were on the 4th floor and Dr.Tostevin's rooms were on the 5th floor of the same building. Dr.Hetler had me in his room a half hour before my appointment bathing my eyes in ice water. Dr.Tostevin praised me as acceptable for air crew and I received my notice of call up to be given a date. This started my Air Force career as an Australian Navy leading Aircraftsman.

The Japanese entered the war on the 7th of December 1941. Japan attacked Pearl Harbor without warning and brought them and the USA into hostilities. All leave was cancelled and we started digging trenches to repulse the Japs. What we were supposed to use to repulse them was never advised. For as previously advised, we had one operational gun. Still, it was a good exercise and kept us fit.

I finished the course as a qualified D/R Navigator on September 8, 1942 and was allowed two weeks of leave. I stayed at the St Vincent.

I did some surfing and fraternizing with Leah, Mart, or Dorothy, depending on which one had leave at the same time.

I received my commission-Pilot Officer on November 12, 1942. I went on leave just before Christmas 1942. I said farewell to family and friends and was sent to the embarkation depot (show grounds) in Melbourne, Australia. I was awaiting posting to New Guinea or Britain. We continued drill and lectures through early part of January 1943.

On Friday the 15th of January 1943 at 3:30pm, I was called into the Commanding Officer's office and advised I had been appointed adjutant on a ship due to embark from Port Melbourne on the 16th. I was sworn to secrecy and could not tell my friend, John Mann, of my appointment. I had a sad farewell before being whisked away in a car to the ship. What a shock, 36,000 ton ship originally luxury passenger S.S. America converted to a troop ship which carried in excess of 2000 personnel and renamed P23 or S.S. West Point. My staff distributed liberty leave passes only to find that on docking all leave is cancelled. We had a riot on our hands which eventually partly calmed down. Then, the medical officer reports that he has a pilot officer who has contracted venereal disease and has to be placed in the hospital in Auckland, New Zealand.

It was my duty to escort him off the ship and on going down the gangplank listening to the "boos" of all my mates. I returned four hours later to the ship after a nice steak ashore. Our visit to Auckland, New Zealand is to pick up American GI's who have been wounded at Guadalcanal or on leave to return to America. Now, we are really crowded in and gambling starts in a big way. We naturally had no control over the yanks, but forced out members to gamble with them below the deck. After the ninth (9) day at sea we crossed the International Date Line (two Wednesdays in the one week). The Royal Australian Air Force boys in Melbourne had not allowed for this as we were paid weekly not daily, we missed one day's pay (8 day week).

Sunday January 31, 1943 we dock at San Francisco. After four hours my staff with John Mann etc. had sorted out the 1500 personnel into what we had considered the correct groups and we disembarked by train at 1300 to Vancouver, Canada and the balance to Boston, Massachusetts.

We the officers are in a "Pullman" sleeper as seen in American films with Negro train stewards. I wake up in the morning to see my first snow. I had never left Adelaide to see any snowfields in Australia. At any stop we got out and played in the snow like kids. Arrive in Vancouver at midday to temperature -15 degrees and we had not been issued with woolen underclothes. Change trains to Canadian Pacific Railway (a magnificent train). Before boarding we have to issue blankets to the L.D.C.'s. Drop L.C.D.'s off at various camps enroute such as Calgary and Winnipeg etc. We dropped the last of our L.D.C's at Montreal after two feet thick snow. The temperature was -25 degrees.

Prince Edward Island is the home of the Silver Fox (main industry for coats). This is an embarkation depot for transfer to the United Kingdom. Prince Edward still had prohibition, only drinks available in the Mess. In spare time we played our first game of ten pen bowling. John Mann was the champion. The cold affected the Australians so much that we found it impossible to go from sleeping quarters to classrooms without stopping to any available building to partly thaw out. The cold makes your head feel as though a red hot band is around your forehead. I started getting severe nose bleeds. As we were now in the Northern Hemisphere we have to learn all our Astro Navigation again. All the stars are different, for example: no midnight on March 15, 1943.

After a lot of parades and route marches we were advised of our embarkation which would be in convoy number fifteen. We joined an 8 knot convoy (we eventually find out of 65 ships) John and I in the Beaverhill going across the Atlantic. We embarked on the Beaverhill on March 27, 1943. A 8000 ton cargo passenger ship with only a few cabins. The convoy is attacked by a pack of U-Boats. One U-Boat surfaces in the middle of the convoy and fires torpedoes and a tanker two ships from ours is blown up. We are attacked for four days and nights and the convoy is forced to scatter and we see ships being blown up all around us. We have to stay day and night in full dress (no pajamas) and wear a life belt for twenty four hours of each day. The couple of Corvettes escorting us were dashing around dropping depth charges. On April 8 I see my first Sunderland Flying Boat which had come out from Ireland to escort us. We sight the coast of Ireland (first land since Canada) and eventually sail into the straits between Ireland and England on our way to debarkation in Liverpool.

We pass close to a mine and a naval vessel dashes in and sinks the mine. Friday, April 9, 1943, we partied in the ships lounge after tea. Then, we pass the Isle of Mann and Berth in Liverpool. We stepped on British soil at 4:00pm on April 10, 1943. We attended a dance that was held in a reception hall of the British Council. Now, we learn what a real blackout looks like. Several days of parades, lectures, and route marches and we are then advised of our postings.

Des, Ross, Keith, and I were assigned to flying boats and poor John Mann torpedo bombers. We traveled through London and after the short stay, we were off to Scotland to station at No.4 Operational Training Unit Arness (near Invergordon). I joined 201 Squadron (RAF) Navigator- Sunderlands (a flying boat).

Our operational training (regarding the Royal Air Force) is carried out from Scotland to Scapa Floe and up around Norway which is occupied by Germany. We carried out nine flights the main one being an anti-sub patrol of 11.5 hours. On the flight of June 22, 1943 we sighted and attacked a U-Boat.

201 Squadron Castle Archdale, Northern Ireland, 8/7/43: Training is now over and we are in to the serious part of the War. We attend a talk on arrival by our wing commander, Vander Kiste. I fall out immediately when he asks all "Colonials" to stand and

introduce themselves. After lots of gunnery and bombing practice our crew is screened by Wing Commander, Vander Kiste. We go on our first convoy patrol of 16.5 hours (3 hours of night flying). We flew operations every three days each flight between 15 and 17 hours. For recreation we played squash and billiards. Ireland (South) was neutral and was out of bounds to Air force as we could be interned if caught over the border. This did not stop us from getting out of our uniform some evenings, catching a taxi to the border and crossing over into Pettigo, Ireland. Our Ventures went well until a Canadian Squadron joined our station and tried to run whisky across the border. This put Pettigo out of bounds for 2 to 3 months. The Canadians were not popular with the rest of us.

One Sunderland from the Australian Squadron 461 was attacked by 14 German J.U.88's. The armament of Sunderlands' was all in the tail, upper turret and front turret; none were underneath. The Sunderland dived to 500ft. above water to stop J.U.88's from diving underneath. The Sunderland shot down or damaged 8 of the 14 attacking aircraft. Nine of the twelve Sunderland crew were killed and the aircraft was shell riddled with bullets. The crippled Sunderland returned to Pembroke Dock and crash landed on land nearby to stop from sinking.

After a couple of months our Squadron stayed at Castle Archdale but our boat was chosen to join the Australian No.10 Squadron at Plymouth at Mt.Batten. Plymouth No.10 Squadron due to enemy action in the Bay of Biscay had met a lot of enemy attacks from German J.U.88's taking off from France (now occupied). They had lost six of their twelve operational Sunderlands and we were to assist until they built up strength again.

It was our standard crew with Eddy (Badly) Bent as Captain, and then Vander Kiste decided to fly down with us for the operations in "the Bay". He liked our crews performance and although we clashed originally I became his pet navigator, hence his reason for flying with us in a dangerous area. We flew six operations from Mt. Batten during the month of September, 1943. When ten squadron strength built up we returned to Castle Arendale to rejoin our squadron.

During my operational training as bombing leader my other Australian "mate" navigator Jack Gerraud is killed in operations. Of the three Australilian members of 201 I am the only survivor. At this stage as senior navigator I was the first navigator to be offered the position of Captain of the crew. Although it was an honor, I declined. If the navigator is Captain he could be allocated a pilot with very little experience and few operational hours.

I obtained 48 hour leave to meet Ken, Clive, and Jonathan and Sir Stanton Hiers who were over to try and sell Wiles Cookers to the British Army. I spent two nights at the famous Savoy Hotel. I still have a Savoy coat hanger as a souvenir.

On June 8, 1944 flying with W/C Lawrence and S/L Powell as a screen, (instructing) to P/o Little off Brest (France in Bay of Biscay) we were shadowed by 2 J.U.88 twin engine fighters. Our tail and mid upper gunners fired blasts of tracers (night time) and rounds of ammunition. They made runs at our Sunderland but thought better of us and sheared off. No damage. They were probably as scared as we were.

On October 30, 1944 I navigated a Sunderland from Pembroke Dock, Wales in transit with the Squadron, to Castle Archdale, Northern Ireland and this happened to be my last flight in the R.A.F.

I have applied for leave without pay to take a residence in London so that I can negotiate with the British Army and R.A.F. the sale and acceptance of the Wiles Steam Cooker on behalf of our firm. Now, the war has been concentrated on the content. Also, the damage to U Boats by bombing their sub pins in Germany. Our heavy commitment of aircraft and Navy in the North Atlantic had fizzled out the war and my leave was granted. I had flown thirty operational flights of 800 hours in the R.A.F.

**Ivor Wiles**
*(Courtesy of Mark Temme)*

**Morris and Sarah Casey**
*(Courtesy of Morris Casey)*

**Dan McCarthy (bottom left) with Family**
*(Courtesy of Dan McCarthy)*

## *Prelude to Victor's future Korea and Vietnam Book*

Victor I would be honored beyond words of explanation if you were to use my article in your new book. People should know that war doesn't take a break at 5 pm and everybody goes home to dinner for the next day when you pick up the battle where you left off.

I pray that you and Kay are doing well. All is well here. I really enjoyed lunch with you two last year and hope it can happen again soon.

**Earle "Doc" Jackson**
*(Courtesy of Earle "Doc" Jackson)*

God bless you for your recognition of our country's warriors. Stay safe, I have attached a photo of me after completing training to become a paratrooper. The other photo is of combat medic survivors of the Battle for Hill 875 gathering in Memphis in 2008. Talk about diversity, in the photo are, two native-Americans, three White guys, and three African-Americans. We love each other, thanks again God Bless you

Your friend,
Earle Jackson

# 173 Paratrooper Medics

**Earle "Doc" Jackson (2nd from left)**
**Vietnam War, Airborne Medics Reunion**
*(Courtesy of Earle "Doc" Jackson)*

# GIVING THANKS ATOP HILL 875

## Journal by *Earle "Doc" Jackson*
## *173rd Paratrooper Medic*

Two days before Thanksgiving in 1967, three companies of the 173rd Airborne Brigade, about 300 men, moved cautiously forward up the hill known only as Hill 875. It was tough going. The riflemen could only see 10 feet in any direction because of the dense jungle cover.

Charlie and Delta companies were within a couple of hundred yards of the summit. Alpha Company hung back to hack an LZ (landing zone) out of the dense jungle so that choppers could resupply and carry out the wounded, if necessary.

Hill 875 is in Dakto Province, Republic of Vietnam. Dakto was the main exit route for the Ho Chi Minh Trail; just a few miles away was the Cambodian border. It was on this day, in this place, that I, a 22 year-old paratrooper and combat medic from Plainville, Connecticut would forever change the way I think about Thanksgiving Day.

As the two forward infantry companies moved up Hill 875, sniper fire rang out; then mortar fire crashed through the trees. The paratroopers immediately hit the ground for cover and looked forward to return the enemy fire, men were falling in all directions, but there were no enemy targets. That would soon change.

Near the half finished landing zone, Pfc. Carlos Lozada, a young trooper from New York, was the first to make contact with the enemy as he covered his Alpha Company's move uphill and away from the LZ.

Alpha company was trying to join up with Charlie and Delta companies further up the hill but were pinned down by brutally intense enemy fire.

Lozada stayed behind and fought off more than 50 advancing

North Vietnamese soldiers. He was last seen on his knees, covered with his own blood, still firing his M-60 machine gun from the hip until he ran out of ammunition. On that day Lozada earned the Medal of Honor for his bravery but lost his life in the process.

The battle for Hill 875 was now under way and, for the next 50 or so hours, the tide of the battle would turn again and again. There was little water and no food, but the men hung in there, the living fighting for their lives next to the growing number of dead.

Then the worst possible thing happened. An American Marine Sky Raider missed its target, dropping a 500-pound bomb that crashed through the trees. Instantly 20 paratroopers were killed, including our beloved brigade chaplain, Maj. Charles Watters.

Chaplain Watters didn't have to be in the jungle, on top of the hill, but he always insisted on being up front where his men needed him most. He died comforting and praying over wounded and dying paratroopers. Chaplain Watters was posthumously awarded the Medal of Honor for bravery under fire.

The North Vietnamese commanders sent wave after wave of fresh troops firing downhill at the paratroopers. The noise was deafening. The intense fire never let up and it was taking its toll.

Most of the officers were now dead or wounded and almost all of the medics were dead.

Reinforcements finally arrived from the 173rd base camp a few miles away; air strikes and artillery kept the enemy off guard and in their bunkers, but the continuous pounding had little effect on the 10-foot-thick bunker covers constructed by the North Vietnamese.

Like every God forsaken enemy-held hill in Vietnam, Hill 875 could only be taken one way and that was one bunker line at a time; this would eventually require men to face off against men. Before this battle was over many more brave men would suffer and die.

The troopers, now into their second night on Hill 875, continued to hold their ground. No one slept that night; the silence was occasionally broken by the wounded crying out in pain.

There is something gut-wrenching about severely wounded men that I will never forget, and that is almost all become delirious and almost always cry out for their mothers. The scores of wounded could not be evacuated because of the heavy enemy fire. They would have to stay on the hill for the night; many died in the cold night air from their unattended wounds.

On Thanksgiving Day morning, the order came down to move up and take Hill 875. At one point, the firing was so heavy it took almost four hours to move 50 meters.

Hill 875 was finally taken. With the hill secured, the battalion commander ordered hot turkey dinners brought up by chopper from our base camp a few miles away. After all it was Thanksgiving Day. The troopers sat quietly, filthy and exhausted from not having slept in two and a half days.

As the sun set on the now barren hill, atop the bunkers that had been occupied by enemy soldiers just hours before, we sat and ate our Thanksgiving dinner in silence. Some men were just too shaken to eat; others couldn't keep the food down in spite of their hunger.

When I look back, it wasn't much of a holiday; 110 brave young paratroopers died taking Hill 875, and about 200 hundred more were wounded.

On Thanksgiving Day I enjoy my dinner and my family, but I will forever think of men like Lozada, medics Rigsby and Hester, and many others less fortunate than myself who gave their lives on Hill 875.

If you have trouble finding something to be thankful for this Thanksgiving holiday, be thankful that you were not on Hill 875 Thanksgiving Day in 1967.

*Airborne All the way!*

Earle "Doc" Jackson
*Combat medic in Vietnam with the*
*173rd Airborne Brigade, 1967-68*

# SELECTED REFERENCES

1. *These Hallowed Halls,* by Andrew Gonzales, FSC and Alejandro Reyes, Manila, De La Salle University, 1982.

2. *The War : An Intimate History 1941-1945,* Geoffrey C. Ward and Ken Burns, Alfred A. Knopf, New York, 2007.

3. *Scenes From the End,* Frank E. Manuel, Steerforth Press, South Royalton, Vermont, 2000.

4. *Pacific War,* John Costello, New York, NY, 1982.

5. *Medal of Honor,* by the Congressional Medal of Honor Foundation, Singapore, 2006.

6. *The Simon and Schuster Encyclopedia of World War II,* Cord Communications and Thomas Parish, New York, NY, 1978.

7. *Journals of Howard Lee.*

8. *I'm a "MAD-CAT" Journal* by Howard Lee.